CHICAS ON THE
APPALACHIAN TRAIL

Women-Specific Tips for Thru-Hiking the
Appalachian Trail and Conversations with
Badass Women Hikers

JEN BECK SEYMOUR

TABLE OF CONTENTS

I. INTRODUCTION

"I know I hike like a girl.
Try to keep up."

~UNKNOWN

When I was a kid, I read the entire series of Trixie Belden books. My favorite place to read was high up in a tree in the vacant lot next to our house. It was actually two trees that had grown together with sturdy branches throughout, and I could just reach the first branch if I jumped and hoisted myself up like a gymnast. I'd stuff the latest volume of Trixie's adventures along with an apple in my pockets and climb high to a comfortable perch where I could view my whole neighborhood.

The more I read about Trixie, the more I wanted to be a tomboy just like her (this was the first time I had heard of such a thing). Trixie had a cool name and a sassy haircut. She was smart – she solved mysteries! *How cool,* I thought, *to be a girl – but to also be strong, feisty, confident and athletic like a boy – a girl who could hold her own while hanging with the guys.*

But it was hard being a tomboy all the time. I also liked wearing ribbons in my hair, playing with my Barbie dolls, wearing lip-gloss, and talking to my girlfriends about dreamy Shawn Cassidy while sitting in my pink canopied-bedroom.

I watched my three younger brothers closely for any clues they could give me about being boy-like. This is what I discovered – they loved camping, fishing, anything to do with dirt and mud, playing with spiders and snakes, and living in the woods for days at a time.

Me? Not so much. The very thought of being dirty and not showering for days, sleeping uncomfortably on the ground, and possibly encountering a thousand and one creepy-crawlies just didn't do it for me.

Some tomboy I was. I wanted all the power and glory of being a tomboy without the dirty work.

Despite my lack of enthusiasm for camping, fishing, or wrestling in the mud, I did learn to hang with the boys. I could run, bike, skateboard, and play basketball and tackle football with the best of the guys in my neighborhood.

Little did I know then that I didn't *need* to be a tomboy to be strong, athletic or confident – I could be all those things and smart to boot, all while wearing pigtails and a skirt!

Nine-year-old me, cruising on my skateboard

But I certainly know it now! In 2017, I lived in the woods for half a year while thru-hiking the entire Appalachian Trail with my husband, Greg (trail name: Sunsets). We trekked over 2,000 miles from Georgia to Maine.

MY THRU-HIKE WAS AMAZING!

I didn't wear make-up or do my hair, and yet I felt beautiful.

I worked my body hard, usually all day long, and slept soundly every night.

I lost 38 pounds while eating whatever I wanted and as much as I could!

I felt awake, vivacious, alert, and ready to go every morning (well, most mornings). Each day was new: new terrain, new mountains to climb, and new vistas to gaze at serenely.

I didn't shower for days at a time but rarely noticed my

stench.

I slept each night in my tent, next to my equally grimy husband, but felt more connected to him than ever (and since we're all girls here, I can share with you that I had some of the best sex of my life while on the trail!).

I wasn't the fastest hiker, but I have never felt stronger. My legs were incredible machines – these two limbs carried and transported me over 2,000 miles, walking 20-plus miles a day, up and down mountains, through roots and rocks and streams. As my hike went on, my calf and thigh muscles fully developed and my back-of-thigh, cottage-cheese cellulite vanished completely.

Though I was tired and hungry all the time, I also felt energetic with mad rushes of adrenaline.

Although I'm 90% introverted and wasn't focused on making friends, I ended up connecting with numerous incredible people, with whom I am still friends to this day. I especially loved meeting other women and girls on the trail, who ranged in age from one to 69.

I am still astounded at what I accomplished.

Completing a thru-hike of the Appalachian Trail was probably the most challenging experience of my life and one of the best adventures I've ever had.

When I first heard of the Appalachian Trail (AT), I only associated it with the male species. The first person to thru-hike the AT was Earl V. Shaffer in 1948. However, the first female to thru-hike the AT came just four years later in

1952. Most people think this was Grandma Gatewood, but in fact it was Mildred Norman, who completed the thru-hike with her husband. She was known as the "Peace Pilgrim" and went on to log over 25,000 miles across North America throughout her life, all in the name of peace.

And you may have heard of Emma "Grandma" Gatewood, who (at the age of 67 in 1955) was the first woman to thru-hike *solo*. In 1964, she became not only the first woman but the first *person* to complete the AT three times. She became something of a celebrity, and thank goodness she did. Her fame brought much needed attention to the trail, instigating maintenance and reconstruction which may not have happened otherwise.

In spite of Gatewood's accomplishment, hiking the AT is still a male-dominated sport. Even so, I was impressed with the number of women I saw in 2017, when only a few years before I read that only one out of five hikers were women, and 10 years ago, only one out of 10. As of 2018, the thru-hiker percentage of female hikers on the AT is around 30%.

Almost three million people (male and female) hike some part of the Appalachian Trail each year. Most are day hikers, multi-day hikers, or "LASH'ers" (long-ass section hikers), but only a small fraction of those hikers (25-30% of women and men combined) complete the entire Appalachian Trail in one 12-month period and earn the title of "thru-hiker."

I chose *Chica,* a Spanish word for "girl" or "woman," as my trail name (a nickname used on a thru-hike) for two reasons. When I moved to Costa Rica, I had a blog and wrote a book, both entitled *Costa Rica Chica.* But when I chose my trail name, Chica became even more meaningful to me. I was proud to participate in a predominately male playing field and to attempt a hike of 2,200 miles over rugged terrain. Hiking like a girl – a chica – sounded like the most badass thing I could do.

I became the tomboy I always wanted to be yet still retained my femininity. Yes, I was a girl – I wore braids and sometimes a skort (skirt with shorts underneath), and I shaved my legs occasionally – but I was also a strong hiker, becoming more fit and capable every day. I could literally climb a mountain, take a rest, and then climb another mountain, and another, and another. Instead of wondering whether or not I could do this, I became aware of just how much I could do. When I summited Mount Katahdin at the end of my hike, I not only fulfilled a huge dream, but I also discovered my own power to take on seemingly insurmountable challenges.

47-year-old me, thru-hiking the Appalachian Trail

CHICAS ON THE APPALACHIAN TRAIL is not meant to be a comprehensive guide; rather, it is more focused on female-specific, long-distance hiking interests. Let's face it, women have completely different body parts, as well as different concerns, fears and questions, than men. For a more general overview and tips for successfully thru-hiking the AT, check out *Thru-Hiking the Appalachian Trail – 100 Tips, Tricks, Traps, and Facts*, which my husband and I wrote together.

In *CHICAS ON THE APPALACHIAN TRAIL*, we will go over everything relating to women hikers: fears and safety concerns, gear tips and suggestions, budgeting parameters, personal hygiene topics (including peeing, pooping, periods and sex). And my favorite part – interviews with 12 badass women who have hiked the Appalachian Trail and who share their thoughts, advice and secrets. I want all my fellow *chicas* to have as much information as possible to help you prepare for a successful thru-hike!

At the end of this book you will find an Appendix, which has a list of typical slang terms used by the thru-hiking community. Beginning in chapter one, the first use of each term will appear in quotation marks with a brief parenthetical definition.

Hiking the Appalachian Trail – in part or in whole – can be empowering and life-altering. Being fully armed with information about specific issues which you as a woman will face on the trail will set you up for victory on this epic journey.

II: WOMEN-SPECIFIC CONCERNS

"Fear, to a great extent, is born of a story we tell ourselves, and so I chose to tell myself a different story from the one women are told. I decided I was safe. I was strong. I was brave. Nothing could vanquish me."

– CHERYL STRAYED, *Wild*

So you're thinking of thru-hiking the Appalachian Trail, but now you have a thousand questions, starting with *why am I doing this?* Let's first talk about the why, and then we'll dive into the plethora of potential experiences that cause anxiety for many women considering a long-distance hike. Knowing what problems you might encounter and researching solutions before they happen will increase your chance of success. Forewarned is forearmed.

1. WHY THRU-HIKE THE AT?

A long-distance hike is not for everyone. In fact, a very low percentage of the population even think of thru-hiking the AT in the first place. But those who consider hiking it have several reasons for doing so.

One of the best parts of hiking the AT is that the terrain changes daily – you never know what you're going to see or hike through each day. It could be a field, a forest, an easy path, or roots, boulders, even mountains. You have a guidebook, but you don't know what the trail or views actually look like until you get there, so each day is a new adventure.

Many people attempting a thru-hike are experiencing a major life change – such as graduation, divorce, retirement – and need or want an adventure to bring their lives into focus.

I was going through a transition before my hike – I had moved back to the US from Costa Rica and was not ready to settle down. I was ready for a new adventure – a new challenge – and since my husband and I enjoy hiking and being outdoors, it was time to take our sport to the next level. Quite simply, I wanted to do something badass.

One woman recently told me that she was sick of hearing from her doctor that some ailment is "typical for a woman of your age." She refused to let her age define her, telling me, "My age?! I don't want to be typical! I want to thru-hike the Appalachian Trail!"

Indeed, there is no age limit for women who want to hike

long-distance. At the time of publication, the oldest woman to thru-hike the Appalachian Trail was 74 (trail name, Drag'n Fly, in 2014). If you're older than 74, go for it – and break the record while you're at it.

On the other end of the age spectrum, I met Kanga in 2017 (you will meet her in Chapter 16) who thru-hiked with her husband and their under-one-year-old baby girl, Roo. Roo became the youngest person to traverse the Appalachian Trail (I say *traverse*, as she was carried on the backs of her parents and didn't hike under her own power).

Whatever your reasons for considering a thru-hike, the benefits are numerous. The physical challenges will strengthen your body and you will be proud, not only at what you accomplish each day, but also of your increasing fitness. You will be amazed at what your body can do. Spending your days in the freshness of the outdoors, seeing things most people will never see – a moose drinking from a pond, a bear noshing on berries, a sunrise over a secluded lake hidden in the woods – can renew your spirit and help you deal with the struggles you may have experienced. Getting away from the stresses of your life (family, work, personal tragedy, politics) and living in the relative peace and quiet of the woods will help you clear your head and get to know yourself better so you can make those important decisions about the next phase of your life. You will also form friends of all kinds and ages. You will bond over the simple act of hiking every day, all day.

There are no societal parameters in the woods. Your profession doesn't matter, nor does your skin color, age or gender. We are all hikers. I was 47 when I hiked the trail, but

I hung out with 20-year-olds sometimes and considered them friends. They didn't treat me like a mom, and I didn't treat them like children. I also made friends with people my age and older. What we had in common was a shared, intense experience.

The AT takes both mental and physical stamina, and I sincerely believe that if you can do it, you will have the confidence, strength, and courage to tackle whatever challenges you face in the future.

Why NOT take a hike in the woods?

JEN BECK SEYMOUR

2. SAFETY

I belong to several online groups for women hikers, and I see posts almost daily from women who are absolutely petrified by hiking-related fears. But because of their strong desire and love of hiking, along with the support of other women, their anxieties soon diminish. Many find themselves invigorated by what they can accomplish – especially once they get out on the trail and push past their fears.

I want not only to make you aware of some of the particular concerns women have, but also to alleviate your worries. Don't forget: women have been hiking the AT for years – and most of them do so as solo hikers.

Worrying about safety and potential problems, though, is actually a good sign. Why? Because it means you will do extensive research on everything that could go wrong, find solutions, and formulate a plan of action for each situation.

My secret weapon is something I call the "positive power of negative thinking." I used this technique to prepare myself to leave behind my familiar, mundane, working life in Texas, for an exotic life of adventure in Costa Rica, and to prepare for taking on the AT.

First, I research and find out about any and all challenges I might encounter. Next, I imagine each of those situations *actually happening* to me (sounds negative, right?). I then investigate further to find acceptable ways to cope *when and if* they occur.

For example, before my husband and I moved to Costa Rica,

I heard over and over about how awful the rainy season was – flooded roads, mudslides, water shutoffs, power outages, *etc.* So I imagined each scenario and came up with a plan in my head for what I would do when it happened. As it turned out, crazy things did happen in the rainy season in Costa Rica, but we were prepared to handle them all.

And while prepping to hike the AT, I learned about foot problems, injuries, bears, hypothermia, lethargy, ticks, river crossings, heat stroke, *etc.* Sunsets and I imagined each of these scenarios aloud, talked them through, and came up with plans for how to deal with them. In this way, none of the situations that happened to us were scary – we had already imagined them and were ready for them.

Oh, and if those problems don't occur? EVEN BETTER. Glass half-empty becomes the glass totally full.

And with that, my friends, you are armed and ready to take on the Appalachian Trail. You can shift your fearful energy into positive excitement for your hike. Be confident that whatever happens, you already have a course of action for dealing with it. You will be better equipped to help others as well.

Let's dive into some real fears women have about thru-hiking the AT and look at statistics and solutions that may help alleviate those fears.

MURDERS

When Bill Bryson published *A Walk in the Woods: Rediscovering America on the Appalachian Trail* in 1997, there were a total of nine known Appalachian Trail murders since 1974. According to AppalachianTrailHistory.org, to date, there have been a total of 11 Appalachian Trail murders (only two more in 21 years). As Bryson succinctly stated:

"Look, if you draw a two thousand-mile-long line across the United States at any angle, it's going to pass through nine murder victims."

This may initially sound like a high number, but if you take into account that 2-3 million people hike a portion of the Appalachian Trail every year, this is actually an extremely low number. Chances are much higher for you to be murdered in the city you live in, rather than along the 2,000-plus miles on the AT.

STRANGER DANGER

The first line of defense is identifying who might be a threat in the first place. Overall, the AT is a very safe place and hikers rely on each other for support, information, and camaraderie. And this reliance often happens within minutes of meeting someone.

While you are on trail, particularly if you are hiking by yourself, be smart about your surroundings and others you may meet. Most fellow thru-hikers are good people, but as you know, there will be a few bad eggs out there, no matter where you are.

You're more likely to encounter troublesome people within a mile or two of road crossings, and these people are typically not thru-hikers or any type of hiker at all.

Dr. Mary Ellen O'Toole, a retired FBI profiler, has written

Dangerous Instincts: How Gut Feelings Betray Us, in which she lists some behaviors to look for that may signify a dangerous person:

• Impulsivity

• Tendency toward angry outbursts and excessive holding of grudges

• Narcissism (extreme selfishness, a grandiose view of one's talents, a craving for admiration from others)

• Lack of empathy

Keep in mind that these characteristics can be found in almost anyone, but if someone displays any of these traits when you first meet them, be aware that they *may* be dangerous. For example, when a stranger exhibits inappropriate anger during your earliest encounters, you should recognize that behavior as odd and potentially violent.

Also, pay attention to people who don't "fit in" or don't "look right." You will quickly come to distinguish thru-hikers and day hikers from non-hikers. Of course, they may have a very good reason for being on the trail, but then again, they may not. Be on alert and wary of anyone who does not look like a hiker or official trail personnel.

How to avoid trouble before it begins: Try not to engage in conversation with people who appear out of place. Be polite and brief. If they say "hi," say "hi" back, avert your gaze, and keep walking. Put distance between you.

What to do if attacked: Your main line of defense is always to avoid trouble in the first place. But if you are attacked by someone, you need to fight and fight hard – with everything you've got. Remember, you are fighting for your life!

What follows are the main steps in putting your attacker out of commission – at least long enough for you to run away:

• If the attacker is male, knee him as hard as you can in the groin.

• Stomp on the instep of his foot – again, as hard as you can.

• Go for your attacker's eyes and try to rip or gouge them out. This is not a time to be timid!

There are also alarm devices that you can have handy on your backpack which could be loud enough to scare your attacker away and could also alert other hikers in the area.

TROUBLESOME MEN

One of the top contenders for "what women fear most on a solo hike" are troublesome men. Most of the guys I met on my thru-hike were decent, well-behaved men, and you will probably find this is true on your hike as well. But as with everyday life, you will meet some guys on the trail who present challenges for you.

Some guys are just jerks. You know them – the men who belittle you or try to "mansplain" (explain something in a condescending way). Every woman has probably experienced some form of this from a man at one point or another. But guess what? Men like this are usually insecure. It's not you, it's them.

I'm not sure what the best way to handle this type of person is, but I can tell you what I did. I didn't waste my time or energy getting into an argument with them. I chose to be amused by them, interrupted their mansplaining as soon as I could, thanked them for their advice with maybe a bit of a smirk on my face, and headed on my way.

Then there are the creepy guys. These are guys who may not say anything specifically but who simply give off a creepy vibe. Sure, they could be totally harmless, but you just never know, and better to be safe than sorry.

Do what you would normally do when you get a creepy vibe. The problem is you are in the wilderness with fewer people and potentially a long way from civilization. Try not to engage in conversation, make minimal eye contact (although seeing what they look like or are wearing is good, in case you need to report them), walk away and find other hikers as calmly and as soon as possible. Depending on the situation, report the person to the police – if this person was creepy enough to scare you, you don't want him scaring anyone else either.

Almost all of the men and boys I met in the six months it took me to hike the trail were great guys. Many of them are now my good friends. So if you promise to remember that almost all hiker guys are cool, I will tell you about the two times I got the creeps on the trail.

The first time was at a shelter about one mile off trail. There were two older, rough-looking men in the shelter who did not look like hikers – they wore clean military fatigues and their backpacks were huge. They both made eye contact with me several times but didn't say anything. They did not smile, just stared. Sunsets felt the same (I found out later) and we didn't stay long but went a good distance away from the shelter to set up our tent. We never heard anything more about them, and when we left the next morning, they were already gone.

The second time occurred when we arrived at a crowded shelter and campsite. We found a flat spot and put our packs down and started putting up our tent. All of a sudden, a guy came running down the hill towards us, yelling that we were taking his tent site. Even though he had left nothing at the site to claim it (as any other hiker would do), he was livid that we were taking "his" spot. His agitation, along with his wildly excited, wide-eyed stare, put my husband and I on high alert – it just wasn't typical hiker behavior. And he wasn't merely upset – he kept making accusations.

So how should you respond in this kind of situation? Instead of being confrontational, we calmly apologized and told him no worries, we would move. That is the BEST thing to do in that situation – know when you might be dealing with a volatile person, apologize, be respectful, treat them as if they are 100% right and you are wrong, and then remove yourself as soon as possible. Had we insisted on remaining, I am certain his attacks would have escalated from verbal to physical.

What about stalkers? "Pink blazing" can be an amusing flirtation as a man chases or tracks a woman on the trail by reading her log entries at shelters. Likewise, women sometimes track men in the same way ("banana blazing"). As long as both parties are enjoying it, it's a cute thing that can happen between thru-hikers. Be aware of it and know that pink (or banana) blazing can cross the line between flirting and stalker-like behavior.

LGBTQ-FRIENDLY

How friendly is the trail for the LGBTQ community?

We met Roar and Sushi Roll, a married couple, early in our hike, and ran into them so often that we considered them part of our tramily. I felt a kinship with them as they were from my home state of Wisconsin and seemed to have thoroughly researched thru-hiking. (I love fellow planners!) Both Sunsets and I enjoyed hiking and hanging out with them. Here's what Roar had to say about hiking the AT as a gay couple.

In the thru-hiking community, I felt accepted and safe, especially once I got to see familiar faces and got to know some hikers. I felt like being a lesbian wasn't an issue.

At first when we started our AT hike, Sushi Roll and I were apprehensive about putting it out there that we were gay and married. Not because we were ashamed, but because you never know what someone's reaction could be and we didn't want an awkward moment, judgment or discrimination. We were careful in small towns and in hostels – whether we needed to be or not.

Early on, Sushi Roll and I met a new group of hikers, and one of them asked how we knew each other. Sushi Roll said we started the trail together and we both live in Wisconsin. And I know she said it to avoid that awkward moment or judgment, but it upset me because she didn't say our truth that we're married. So right after she said that, I said, "Oh, and we're married." There was a moment of silence and then it was all fine! Sometimes I think we create our own tension out of not wanting to make things awkward for others.

Anyway, the next day we ended up meeting Mystic, and Sushi Roll (bless her, knowing that I was upset by the way she had referred to us earlier) just straight away introduced us by saying, "I'm Sushi Roll and this is my wife, Roar!" And boom, it was all good.

The further along the trail we got, the more comfortable I became, and being gay and a woman was not an issue. I would have felt safe hiking alone if things had been different (thankfully they weren't because it was awesome hiking it with my love!).

I was totally blown away by the kindness and respect that hikers, especially the thru-hiking community, give all people. At least that was my experience.

Sushi Roll & Roar, Jenkins Shelter, Virginia – AT 2017

Sunsets and I agree that thru-hikers do not care about other thru-hikers' personal lives outside of the AT. They only care about hikers as friends with whom they share a common interest in hiking. That's all that seems to matter on the AT. The rest of the world, and thankfully all its troubles, fall by the wayside. You will find more acceptance on the AT than in everyday life, but as always, use caution and be observant.

INJURIES

On a thru-hike, you will be in the wilderness, lumbering up and down mountains, climbing over rocks, and negotiating wet roots for up to 10 hours a day, every day. It is probable you will fall, have a strain, or otherwise injure yourself in some manner.

There is a wide spectrum of injuries that can occur on the trail – knee, ankle and foot injuries being the most common. It's almost easier to trip and fall on the trail than it is to walk.

Knowing what a klutz I am in everyday life, I can't tell you how worried I was that I would trip in the first week, fall flat on my face, and take myself out of the game before it even began. I even tallied how many times I fell each day in my journal – that is, until it became too hard to count my numerous falls each day. I mean, who would even want to know that I fell eight times in one day? Consequently, I kept my eyes glued to the ground at *all times*. The second I would glance up and look at something, I'd trip. It got to be ridiculous. I actually can't believe that I didn't seriously injure myself with tripping or falling throughout my whole hike.

If you have an emergency injury while on trail, what do you do?

• Check if you have cell service. Try calling 911. Many parts of the trail are accessible by off-road rescue vehicles.

• Stop hiking, do what you can for your injury (clean up, bandage, elevate, *etc.*), and wait for another hiker to come along to help. You may find out you are not too far from the next road gap, and hiker friends could help you hobble out to it.

• Call your insurance company. Trip or rescue insurance is an available option for your thru-hike, which may give you or your family more peace of mind. Do your research. Several insurance companies specialize in hiking and backpacking insurance (*e.g.,* Adventure Consultants, Allianz Global Assistance, Visitors Coverage Travel Insurance Solutions).

• If you have a GPS tracking device, you can text (and sometimes even call) for help, even if there is no cell service in the area. You can also contact your family and possibly have them look up your location, see what you're close to, what help is close by, *etc.*

One woman raved about her Garmin device for her long-distance hike, saying it gave her great comfort. Depending on what model and service you choose, options can include texting, adding waypoints, maps, mileage tracking, and an S.O.S. feature.

Here are a few before-you-go tips:

• Always carry a first aid kit when you hike – even on a day hike.

• Always hike with a guidebook, trail app, compass and maps. Study them before each leg of your hike so you know what to expect.

• You should take overnight gear – even on a day hike – in case you get stuck and have to spend the night.

• Take your cell phone. You can put it on airplane mode to enjoy nature, but you will have it for an emergency if need be. There are also quite a few trail apps or maps you can download to your phone ahead of time.

• Take a Wilderness First Aid course. They are taught throughout the country and only take one weekend to complete. There is also a more intensive two-week course called Wilderness First Responder.

• Remember, being prepared is everything! You will feel more confident and not freak out if something happens.

ILLNESSES

Contracting an illness or disease is also a safety concern on a thru-hike. Many can be prevented with proper water filtering and treatment, good hygiene, attention to not sharing food, and tick checks.

Water. Tainted water is the main culprit in causing illnesses on the trail. Symptoms may include vomiting, diarrhea and intense stomach cramping. Two of the most common contaminates found while hiking are the protozoa *Giardia* and *Cryptosporidium*. Bacteria such as *Salmonella* and *E. coli* can be a problem as well. And finally, there are viruses to contend with. Filtering and treating your water will help prevent these illnesses (see Chapter 10 for methods on filtering and treatment).

Hygiene. Good hygiene is another important practice for remaining disease-free. This means cleaning your hands as best you can after using the bathroom (I mean, the privy or woods) – usually with wet wipes and/or hand sanitizer. According to the LNT (Leave No Trace) guidelines, you can use biodegradable soap like Dr. Bronner's, but do so sparingly and wash at least 200 feet away from water sources. For more information:

http://www.appalachiantrail.org/home/explore-the-trail/leave-no-trace

Food sharing. Do not share your food with other hikers and don't accept food from others. This sounds easy but is actually quite difficult. You may be having lunch with other hikers, having a great time chatting, and the hiker next to you offers you a peanut butter M&M from his bag. Why not take one? Sharing of food is such a social and fun thing to do. However, you don't know where his hands have been, and furthermore if he might happen to be carrying a disease unbeknownst to him. Your hand goes in the bag and touches an M&M that he just touched and – bam! – soon you'll be running for the privy all night long.

Ticks. Of all the animals you may encounter on the trail, ticks are the thru-hiker's biggest nemesis; we'll talk more about this in Chapter 7. Lyme disease, which is contracted from the deer tick, will present itself 70-80% of the time with a circular, bullseye rash. Other symptoms include fatigue, dizziness, problems sleeping, achy or swollen joints, headaches, fever, night sweats, mood changes, and difficulty concentrating. If you suspect Lyme disease, go to a clinic where they can test for it and prescribe a round of antibiotics if the test is positive.

You can treat your clothing with permethrin (either by yourself or have it professionally done), but the best line of defense is to do a tick check every night. There are only a few places you can't see on yourself (head and back). If you are a solo hiker, use your cell phone to take pictures of places you cannot see. Then view the pictures, and only if you see something that could be a tick, ask another hiker for help in removing. Just remember to delete the pictures to avoid an embarrassing situation later.

ANGELS AND MAGIC

Though there will always be dangerous situations in life, whether you are on the trail or in your normal, everyday life, please keep in mind these occasions are extremely rare. You should always be alert to your surroundings and take care of yourself to stay safe, but the majority of people you will meet on the trail are decent people.

In fact, if ever you need your faith restored in humanity, hike the Appalachian Trail and experience the incredible support system of "trail angels." A trail angel is anyone who provides kind assistance ("trail magic") to hikers. Trail magic might appear in the form of a grilled burger or a cold soda at a trailhead, a ride into town, or even a bed at a trail angel's home.

When we were on the trail, a couple following our YouTube videos contacted us to offer us a night's rest in their home. We didn't know these people at all, but they seemed OK from their messages, so we agreed. They picked us up from the trail with ice cold Gatorades. They welcomed us into a beautiful guest suite at their home, brought us drinks while we showered, laundered our clothes, cooked an amazing meal of appetizers and lasagna (plus homemade ice cream!), and provided another fabulous spread for breakfast the next morning before taking us back to the trail. Wow! On top of all that, they were so friendly and fun to talk with, and we have remained friends with them. Believe it or not, this happened more than a few more times. We were blown away by the kindheartedness of people helping thru-hikers.

In real life we are taught not to take things from strangers. But on the trail, accepting help from strangers (unless your gut tells you otherwise) is customary and quite literally refreshing. After your thru-hike, you will remember all the trail angels and their magic for a long time. They are very special people who make a hiker's life much better.

3. FEARS

"Everything you ever wanted is on the other side of fear."

~GEORGE ADDAIR

FEAR OF LONELINESS

Some women worry about living in the woods for several months by themselves. The fact is you will not be alone. Four to six thousand people (increasing annually) attempt to thru-hike the Appalachian Trail every year, so if you want a hiking partner or a "tramily" (trail family), you will find one! It is virtually impossible for you not to meet others on the trail. In my six months on the trail, there were only a handful of days when I did not see anyone else on the trail during the day. I regularly saw people hiking in both directions. Most thru-hikers use shelters and water sources as destination goals, so it is rare not to see other hikers at these locations.

The trail is especially populated for the northbound hiker since the majority hike in that direction and start around the same time of year (any time from late February to late April with March being the most popular time). You may hike alone during the day, but you will most likely pass other hikers when they stop for a break or vice versa. At night, you may choose to stay at the many shelters along the trail – these usually will have a privy, water source, tent sites and sometimes devices for hanging your bear bag. Most hikers, at least in the beginning, stay at or near the shelters.

Your partner or family may also worry about you hiking

alone. Of course, you can call them when you have cell service and stay in contact, but some places on the trail do not have service. Make sure your family is aware of this so they don't assume you are in trouble if you don't call every single night.

Several GPS tracking devices are available that the hiker can wear so someone at home can track them on computer, cell phone, *etc.* A hiker can even send text messages on some tracking devices, even in an area with no cell service.

On the other hand, if you want to be by yourself at night, you will find ample opportunity to "stealth camp." This means setting up your tent away from a shelter. Some of these are shown on the Awol's *Guide* as a tent or campsite while others are not. Stealth sites will typically have a flat, cleared spot for one or more tents and sometimes a fire pit with logs to sit on. You'll need to hang your bear bag; there will not be a privy; and there may or may not be a water source nearby.

You might not suffer loneliness during the day but instead fear sleeping alone in the woods. If you sleep in or tent near the shelters, you will not be alone.

Attie, a fellow thru-hiker I met in 2017, experienced severe loneliness and depression while hiking. She talks about this in Chapter 21 and offers great advice and tips for what she did to overcome this.

FEAR OF HEIGHTS

Acrophobia is a severe fear of heights. I do not have this fear, but my hiking pal, Mystic (whom you will meet in Chapter 22), does, and she shares here how she dealt with her fear on the trail:

I have a gut-wrenching fear of heights, mainly when standing in a wide, open area with no support. Most of the AT is in woods. If I fall, there will be a tree to stop me. However, there are a few places that are open and steep.

This didn't happen often and that part of the trail didn't last long enough for me to become frozen with fear. I became too busy trying to place my next step, figure out whether to use the poles or just drop them down, take off the backpack or leave it on. If there were other hikers, I would try to focus on where they were walking, my sight on their feet and not on the heights. Problem solving kept the fear at bay. Heights did not stop me from hiking.

Sometimes alternate trails are available for you to consider.

Tips:

• Don't hesitate to share your fear with other hikers. They may have similar feelings that you could discuss, or you could help each other, possibly by hiking together.

• Spend time and research to find the right gear for you. Stable shoes with good grips, a pack that fits you well and is centered on your back, and trekking poles will help immensely.

• Know what triggers your fear, and have a game plan for what to do when you come upon this situation. If possible, think about and try to eliminate the irrational threats and focus on the real dangers.

• If you're seriously concerned about this, contact a therapist well before your hike. Cognitive therapy might help you.

• Explore meditation and breathing techniques, which have been proven to help reduce stress and anxiety. Avoid quick, shallow breathing on a hike. Instead, take slow, deep breaths from your belly.

• Don't look down! This might be hard to do if you're going down a steep decline. Try to focus on your immediate area – not the length of the decline or any drop-offs. Concentrate on your hands and feet, or as Mystic mentioned, on the feet of the hiker in front of you. A few times in areas that had rebar steps built into the side of a mountain, I turned around and faced the mountain, which seemed to make this easier and less stressful.

• Test any unstable ground with feet or trekking poles first to avoid tripping or falling.

• Do not let other hikers pressure you to move faster. Take your time and try to remain calm.

FEAR OF LIGHTNING STORMS

Let's face it, lightning and thunderstorms can be scary, even when you're not in the woods hiking. Lightning can kill people, but statistics say less than 50 people in the U.S. are killed each year by lightning, and few of these are hikers. Chances are very low that you will be struck by lightning. On the other hand, that doesn't matter much if this is one of your fears; it can still be very scary.

We tried to keep up to date with the weather every day, as we knew if there were thunderstorms in the forecast, the last thing we wanted was to be on top of a bald mountain or above treeline. Regardless of how hard we tried to avoid it, we still got caught in this situation once.

What started out as a beautiful sunny day in New York with boardwalks through grassy fields soon turned into a threatening, overcast afternoon. The trail led to small wooded mountains on repeat – up, down, up, down, up, down. By this time, we knew the "light sprinkles" forecast was wrong, as we now heard thunder getting closer and closer. Right before we broke through the forest to a rocky boulder wall with rebar steps, it started raining HARD.

We were in a type of depression in the woods but wouldn't be for long if we climbed those steps – they went straight up to what we knew was a long, bald ridgeline with no trees. We did not want to be up there in a lightning storm, let alone caught on the metal rebar.

We found a rock under some low-lying trees where Sunsets opened his rain skirt like a blanket, and we sat there holding the skirt over our heads. Staying dry in a windy rainstorm is pretty much impossible, but there we sat, trying. We could do nothing else but wait in the shelter of the trees.

All of a sudden, we heard voices shouting in the wind as another couple came *down* the rebar steps and asked if we were OK. We shouted, "Yes, we're fine," so they hiked on. We assumed they had gotten caught on the ridgeline in the storm and had no choice but to keep hiking. We sat there for what felt like hours, but in reality was only 10 minutes.

The rain finally slowed to a more moderate pouring, and the

thunder and lightning receded in the distance. We slowly climbed the rebar steps and walked across the bare ridgeline as carefully as we could. Even though we took our time, the rocky floor was so slanted and slippery, we both fell several times. But *at least* we did not get struck by lightning.

Shortly before the thunder and lightning storm

Below are some tips on what to do and what not to do (source: http://www.hikingdude.com/hiking-lightning.php).

• Do (always) check the weather when you can. If you know a bad storm is coming and you are scheduled to be on the top of a treeless mountain that day, you can sometimes make other arrangements.

• Do count the seconds between the lightning and thunder. If less than 30 seconds, you need to take shelter (lightning can strike as far as six miles from a thunderhead!).

• Do find a good enclosed shelter (good shelters include a cabin or trail shelter). If you can't find good shelter, stay away from the highest objects: tall trees, mountains peaks, ridges, boulders, hilltops, towers or large metal objects, ski lift towers, fences, *etc.*

• Do find a valley or depression in the terrain with a line of low trees. If you have anything that conducts electricity (metal-framed backpack, trekking poles, *etc.*), put them at least 100 feet away from you. If you are with others, spread out; this will minimize the risk of multiple victims if a direct strike occurs.

• Do go to the lowest place possible if you are above treeline. Make your body as small as possible and sit on something insulated (foam pad) with your legs crossed. And wait.

• Don't seek shelter under a picnic table or tree all by itself (small objects can also attract lightning).

FEAR OF RIVER CROSSINGS AND ROCK HOPPING

Crossing rivers was one of my biggest fears before I started my hike, so I thoroughly researched the main factors that affect crossing safely, such as time of year and weather (current rainfall or how much snow fell the winter before). Fortunately, the only rivers we needed to ford were in Maine late in the summer. I also researched the best shoes for this and picked the Xero ZTrails as my camp shoes – the soles are made out of old tires with good traction, and the shoes attach to your feet very securely so as not to fall off in a fast flowing river. I felt very lucky that, once we got to Maine, we only had to ford three rivers, none of which came up past mid-thigh, and I didn't trip or fall in any of them.

Along with river crossings, some people also fear rock hopping, which is "hopping" from rock to rock to get across a river instead of walking through the water.

My pal, Karen Youngs, who has a severe fear of river crossings and rock hopping, describes her experience:

I don't have a fear of all waters per se, but more so with moving waters – anything with a current that I irrationally think will whisk me away to the ocean never to be seen again. If I can't actually see how deep the water is, that compounds my fear. My fear of rock hopping would not be so bad if Mother Nature would just place the rocks closer together. Also, if they could all be flat, dry, and a good size, that would be most helpful!

The scariest experience I had was with rock hopping while hiking the Franconia Ridge Loop in New Hampshire with my son, Ryan. I'd hiked plenty with Ryan before but had never really had to cross any substantial water.

To my dismay, not long into our hike we came to a water crossing at the base of a waterfall. It was a beautiful spot and I stood on the edge of the water and asked Ryan if there was another way across. His reply? No.

So I stood there for a few minutes and watched several hikers merrily hop from rock to rock across the river as if they were walking on a carpeted floor.

My son is a great teacher and has amazing patience with all things hiking. He hopped across to show me how "easy" it was – even stopping on rocks halfway across to talk to me as I went into "mom mode," panicking that he was going to fall and bash his head open. He then casually rock-hopped back to me and gently encouraged me to start my way across.

I was FREAKING OUT inside. To me, the water was moving at a pretty good pace. I could see it wasn't terribly deep, so I asked Ryan if I could just skip the rocks and walk across. Again, he said no; he wanted me to face my fears. So I got on the first rock and I will tell you exactly what my problem was. I put too much thought into how I need to get to the next rock and that is what dooms me.

So I stood on the first rock and said to myself: This is it. My ridge loop hike is over. Sorry, Ryan, but I must quit now and go back.

Ryan calmly told me to try using my trekking poles for support. Well, that made things worse. As soon as I put my poles in the water, I could feel the strength of the current. Not good. I needed to go about 25 feet to get across. These rocks were wet, sharp and jagged, not made for feet to land on.

What made me finally move to the next rock was purely feeling bad for Ryan and knowing I had to get across to continue on. Also, Ryan promised me that this was the last water crossing (little did I know that was a white lie!).

I managed to make it to the middle of the river crossing, which is where I stopped and stood for 15 minutes thinking, this is the end – I'm stuck here forever. I wasn't sure how I was going to get out of this situation, but then I noticed several happy hikers waiting patiently for me to move so they could get across. The hikers were behind me, and I had Ryan yelling encouragement in front of me. I eventually made it. It was not graceful, but I got across and felt very accomplished afterwards!

Guess what? We had four (FOUR!) more water crossings that day. However, none were as bad as the first one, and by the fourth one, I almost felt like a pro.

I haven't had to rock hop since, so I'm sure when I have to again, it will feel like starting over. I watch Ryan do it and also the ease of him just running down craggy mountains and I'm amazed at how he does it. It's as effortless as breathing to him. I will never be of that caliber. But I am grateful for having an amazing son for a teacher, and if I have to rock hop again, I know it will be with him and he will get me across.

Franconia Ridge Loop 6/14/2017

Ryan's Instagram: Instagram.com/northbound_ryan **Karen's Facebook Page:** Facebook.com/Get-Your-Rocks-On-296742314034111

Tips for river crossings:

• Take time to assess the river and different areas for crossing. You want the shallowest part – which is not always where the trail meets the river.

• If the water depth is above your knees and is moving rapidly, this could potentially be dangerous. If it is too high and moving fast, please rethink crossing. You could camp out and rest, then look at the levels later in the day or the next morning.

• Store anything that could get wet in waterproof or ziplock bags.

• Unclasp your hip belt. In the instance that you do fall in and it is life threatening, you can easily slip off your pack, which will better enable you to swim.

• Sometimes there is an overhead rope to hang onto for stability, but your trekking poles can work even better (as long as the water is not too deep and not moving too rapidly).

• Take your time. Do not pick up your feet; rather, slide them along the river floor very slowly. Test each footing before you put your full weight on it.

• If you fall in and cannot regain your footing to stand up, remain calm. Your immediate concern should be looking at the shore and where you can safely land. If you feel desperate, slip your pack off and let it go so you can swim with both arms to safety.

• If you can't reach shore and the water flow is very swift, put your feet in front of you facing downstream – better for your feet than your head to collide with obstacles.

Don't let your fears debilitate you. Study the facts, learn what other hikers have done before you, and think of outside-the-box ways to conquer your fears. For example: envision yourself living through your fears on the trail and give yourself options of how to overcome them. Then, bump it up a notch. Get out there: be in the woods in a storm, get lonely, hop or ford that river, hike up high with drop-offs on either side of you, and keep going until you get through to the other side of your fear. You will surprise yourself with how capable you are.

4. EMOTIONAL & PHYSICAL ANXIETIES

Successfully completing a thru-hike takes strength and perseverance, but what percentage of a thru-hike is mental, and how much is physical? I've heard anything from 50/50 to 90/10 or vice versa. Bottom line: it's personal – some hikers struggle more emotionally, while others have a harder time physically.

Let's start with some of the emotions you may go through before (or during) your hike.

<u>GUILT</u>

Some women feel guilty about leaving family and responsibilities. Women are typically caregivers – we take care of people and things and get shit done. We care for our spouses, children, parents, in-laws, grandparents, and even friends and neighbors. But often we neglect to take care of the most important person – ourselves.

Remember in Chapter 1 when we looked at the reasons for hiking the AT in the first place? What is *your* reason? What benefit do you expect from your AT adventure? If a thru-hike, or even a section hike, is something you feel would make you more fit, healthier, or stronger emotionally, then take the time to DO IT. Discuss it with your family and make a plan that works for everyone, but don't give up if this is your dream. Once the decision is made and the plans are in place, don't let guilt stop you.

NEGATIVITY

Family negativity can inspire guilt and derail your plans. If you have a partner and/or children, you will obviously need their support as they will have to take care of themselves and the home while you are away. They must be involved in your pre-planning and should fully understand how important this is to you. A loving partner should encourage you to follow your dreams, but planning together ensures your absence does not create hardships for the family. Furthermore, your adventure will set a great example for your children because they can take pride in your accomplishment. Not only will your family also benefit from learning to take of themselves, but you will be able to enjoy your adventure guilt-free with your family cheering you on.

Early reactions from friends and extended family are sometimes negative and can be discouraging. If you think about it, hiking for six months in the woods sounds completely crazy. People need time to wrap their minds around it, so their first reaction may be to tell you they don't think you are capable. They can't imagine it for themselves, so they don't understand how you can. Others may be jealous that you can take that much time from work and family "to go on an adventure." However, hiking the AT is not a luxury vacation or a mere walk in the park. You have dreamed of this, saved for it, planned and trained for it. Their jealousy comes from the fact that they haven't made their own dreams enough of a priority.

Tips: Be ready for heaps of questions. Be patient with your family and friends. Even though you know everything there is to know about your hike, they may have never even heard of the Appalachian Trail. Answering their questions and informing them about what thru-hiking the trail entails may turn their negativity into positivity. The more they understand what you'll be doing and why, the more comfortable (and hopefully supportive) they'll be. Not only can the answer to "why" usher you through low periods on your journey, but it will also help your friends encourage you to stay determined and to succeed.

I was fortunate that everyone I told about my hike encouraged me. Most asked tons of questions, which I was happy to answer. I'm sure some of them didn't think I could do it, but none voiced this concern before my hike.

After Sunsets and I finished our hike, we heard from some family and friends who admitted that they had little confidence that we would make it all the way – but they were so amazed and proud of us that we did.

DOUBTS

Can I do this? The answer depends on your perspective. A positive outlook will definitely make a difference in your thru-hike attempt.

I happen to be a tenacious person with a positive outlook, so my "mental" part was taken care of before I even started. I knew I was determined to finish the whole trail as long as I was physically capable. Luckily, Sunsets felt the same. In fact, we made a pact before we started: pending a catastrophic injury or family emergency, we were hiking all the way to Katahdin!

I knew there would be hard days. And there were. There were several days of tears when I just had a hard time emotionally.

I remember one day as we were climbing Mt. Cube, NH, I felt so depleted. I turned to Sunsets with tears in my eyes and said, "You know what? This is just not fun anymore!" In the middle of the moment, it seemed like the worst thing ever, but after that day had passed, I realized I was still having fun, just not on that particular mountain's ascent. Through all my bad moments, I was never seriously inured, so the option to quit was never on the table.

One book I highly recommend is *Appalachian Trials: The Psychological and Emotional Guide to Successfully Thru-Hiking the Appalachian Trail* by Zach Davis. Zach, who also runs the popular website TheTrek.co, does a great job of focusing on the mental aspects of a thru-hike. It's the only book that I know of that tackles this subject.

Emotional reasons people quit:

• Suffering from too many new challenges

• Missing family/friends/home

• Feeling too alone on the trail

• Not having any fun

Tips:

• Before your hike, research and gain as much knowledge as you can. Watching other thru-hikers' YouTube videos was helpful to me. I loved how honest some of them were. You will see what can happen and envision it happening to you and how you'd handle it.

• On the flip side, consider taking others' advice with a grain of salt. Something that may be right for another hiker might not work for you.

• Know yourself and keep in mind that you are a capable being! Knowing your weaknesses can prepare you to deal with adverse situations so you can bolster your success. You should become more capable and more confident each day and night you spend on the trail.

PHYSICAL FEARS

Am I strong enough to hike over 2,000 miles? Everyone's body is different, but I will tell you that our bodies are amazing machines. I was continually impressed with how hard I pushed my body and how much stronger I became as my hike progressed.

Think about all the women who have done it before you. Old women have done it. Young women have done it. Out of shape women have done it. Women with debilitating fears have done it. Niki Rellon became the first woman to thru-hike with a prosthetic leg!

Should you train before a thru-hike? Some people will actually tell you not to worry about training – just start the trail and that will be your training. While it's true that you cannot completely train for a thru-hike until you are on the ground hiking every day, you can definitely prepare your body by getting in the best shape you can to increase your chances of success.

I started my training while we were living in Costa Rica, which turned out to be the best thing for me. We lived in the Central Valley in the middle of volcanic mountains at an elevation of 4,700 feet. Hiking every morning was our natural stair climber. Before I committed to a thru-hike of the AT, I wanted to make sure that I could hike at least 15 miles in one day. So we set out a gradual schedule and slowly worked up to it. Before I knew it, we were hiking 15 miles with no foot pain or injuries. I then was confident that I could hike the trail.

I really want to tell you that if I have thru-hiked the Appalachian Trail, **you can do it too!** I was 47, out of shape, and very "green" to hiking and overnight camping. I had never camped in a tent more than two consecutive nights in the woods before we started. Part of the allure of a thru-hike for me was the challenge. I knew it would be hard. But I also knew if I accomplished it, I would feel like I could do anything.

Let's talk about body issues. Some women may think they are too fat, out of shape, or just don't look the way a thru-hiker should. First of all, thru-hikers look completely different as far as their bodies go – I've seen some very large people as well as some extremely tiny people on the trail. If you have medical issues, please check with your doctor before taking on a thru-hike of the AT, but otherwise, remember that all hikers (men and women alike) are in the same boat (er, tent). We are all dirty and stinky with odd tan and dirt lines, no matter our size or shape.

Physical reasons people quit:

• Injury

• Illness or disease

• Low energy

• Extreme difficulty or duration (physically incapable of continuing)

• Excessive weight loss (can't ingest enough calories to keep body fueled)

Again, arming yourself with data on why people quit will help you formulate your own game plan to avoid these problems or to deal with them if they happen to you.

Tips:

• Don't despair – you will get your "trail legs." After about a month, a magical thing happens when everyone's fitness level normalizes and they start to get their trail legs. Your legs start carrying you farther and farther each day, seemingly by magic. You can suddenly go up mountains without stopping every 10 steps to catch your breath. Note that the hike overall never gets easier – you are just able to tackle mountains, terrain, and miles easier than before.

• If you can't get as far as you hoped, remind yourself that you can walk at your own pace. You can take breaks when you need to and then keep walking. And you know what? If you don't complete the whole Appalachian Trail in one 12-month period, it's OK! It doesn't mean you are a failure. Doing any part of the Appalachian Trail is hard and badass, my friend.

• Take your thru-hike one day at a time. Look at each day as a simple day hike. You are going out for one day and that is it. Tomorrow is another day hike. Connect all these day hikes together for 180 days, and you have a thru-hike.

• Work up to more miles gradually. I was worried about starting out too fast too soon – something that commonly occurs in fun runs. As soon as the gun goes off, you have so much adrenaline that you burst out of the gate sprinting. But before long, you realize you've expended too much energy too early and may experience pain or injuries or conk out before the end. Working up to something slowly is better than starting at full speed, especially for a thru-hike; going out too fast can doom your entire hike by issuing you a debilitating injury.

Before our thru-hike, we had found in our research that starting our hike with fewer miles and building up gradually was our best chance for success (and it worked!).

Below is my plan for building up our mileage slowly:

• Week 1: 8 miles a day, with a zero day at the end of this week

• Week 2: 10 miles a day, with a zero day at the end of this week

• Weeks 3 and 4: 12 miles a day, with a zero day at the end of each week

• Week 5 and on: 14 *or more* miles a day, with a zero day once a week

This plan worked great for my husband and me; we never got a blister or a serious injury. I can't tell you how many other hikers we saw that got blisters or injuries from starting out with too many miles too soon. Just because we didn't have blisters or injuries does not mean that we weren't in pain or that we didn't have sore feet. Our feet were sore for our whole thru-hike. They were usually OK in the morning after getting warmed up, but come afternoon they would hurt. Every time we took a break and then stood up, we definitely had what is called the "hiker hobble." (By the way, the hiker hobble is also a good way to instantly spot other thru-hikers.)

A much-respected hiker once told me that a non-athlete hiking the AT has a better chance of succeeding than a super fit or in-shape person. Why? The non-athlete will typically start out with low mileage and work their way up to higher mileage slowly, whereas the athlete is overconfident and knows he's already in shape – so he starts out too strong, too fast. He may be in good shape, but there's NOTHING that can train your body for hiking multiple miles with a heavy backpack, day after day – except hiking several miles with a heavy backpack, day after day.

5. THE 4 P'S AND SEX

Peeing, pooping, periods and privies – that's a lot of P words for the female hiker to be apprehensive about. In addition to all those P's, here's a non-P word for you – sex. You may have questions about sex. *Do hikers do it in the woods? In a tent? While they're stinky and dirty and haven't showered for days?* Have no fear, we will conquer all these topics right now.

PEEING

It stands to reason that women are concerned about peeing in the woods. We don't have easy access to an elongated vagina we can just pull out of our shorts, aim with our hand, go pee, shake dry and put back inside. That actually sounds so easy, I'm surprised some men can't do this *while* hiking (do they really need to stop moving to pee?).

Several devices on the market offer you exactly this pee-like-a-man ability. The difference is, unlike the male species, this device is not attached to your body. Most are extremely lightweight, have a carrying case or pouch, and can be easily cleaned. In the interview section, Mystic discusses using one of these and highly recommends it. Here are some popular brands to look for: Pstyle, GoGirl, Venus to Mars, and Peebuddy. My advice is to try some different peeing devices, find one you really like, keep practicing with it in your hiking clothes, and you'll be set before you start the trail!

I decided to go the old-fashioned route. I would find a secluded spot off the trail, brace myself with a log or small tree, pull my shorts and underwear down to my ankles, squat, and pee. I would hold my underwear and shorts with one hand, stretched away from my shoes, to ensure no pee splattered on my clothes. I then used a "pee rag" – a bandana that is used ONLY for spot drying yourself after you pee. I never understood how some women can "shake dry" and be done with it – I would always feel wet and uncomfortable after doing that. The great thing about the pee rag is after you use it, you simply hang it from the backside of your pack and let it dry in the sun. The sun actually bleaches it, and it becomes scent free. I never once smelled mine. Just a word of caution: you might want to check the pee rag after you use it to make sure there is no discharge on it, as this would be visible and noticeable to a hiker behind you (ew!). Also I recommend a dark colored bandana, so if some parts are slightly wet with pee, you can't tell as much as with a light colored one.

I became so comfortable with peeing in the woods, I sometimes would do it even if there was a privy available. Because there was sometimes a line at the privies, running into the woods behind our tent was quicker and much more private.

What about getting caught while peeing? Several women mentioned experiencing this on the AT. They would supposedly hike to a secluded spot off trail, squat and do their business, and all of a sudden would be startled to see another hiker! Not what you want to happen, right?

First of all, make sure you go a ways off the trail, into the woods, preferably behind a big tree or bush. Secondly, make sure you know where the trail goes or where it came from, as it is typically not a straight line and could curve around right to your bathroom spot.

What about getting up to go pee in the middle of the night? If you are one of those people who have to get up in the middle of the night to go to the bathroom, don't dismay. If you are in a shelter, try to put your sleeping bag down close to the open wall so you can easily get out without walking over sleeping hikers in the middle of the night. Most shelters have a privy, so just know where the privy is, have your TP bag ready, and it shouldn't be a problem.

If you are in a tent, hammock, or tarp set-up, pick out a place nearby before you go to sleep at night. It can be pretty close to your tent, as in the dark you don't want to walk too far away, and hopefully, everyone else will be sleeping, so you won't need privacy. Take your headlamp so you will be hands-free. You need to be especially careful of tripping on rocks and roots, and be on the lookout for snakes.

ANOTHER OPTION: With a wide-mouth Gatorade bottle, use your peeing device inside your tent, replace the lid, and empty it in the morning. My husband actually did this (um, without the peeing device) and it worked great for him.

POOPING

Pooping is similar to peeing in the woods. You usually have to squat a bit longer than when you only pee. Also, you will need your "TP (toilet paper) bag" with you. The TP bag should include a trowel, toilet paper, wet wipes if you use them, and hand sanitizer.

Tips:

• Don't go until you really have to! You don't want to be squatting for hours – your leg muscles will not allow for this. You will be fit from hiking every day, but you will also be tired. You do not want your legs to give out and land yourself right in your pile of poo!

• Select a spot at least 70 paces from the trail, water sources or campsites. A support log or tree trunk is helpful. Sometimes when I was in a hurry, I just squatted with my two hands behind me on the ground for support.

• Use your trowel or stake to dig a hole six inches deep.

• Squat and do your business in the hole.

• Use as little toilet paper and/or wet wipes as possible. Toilet paper goes into the hole; wet wipes (even the biodegradable ones) must be packed out.

• Bury your shit (sorry) with dirt.

• Push a stick into the hole so other hikers will know not to dig there.

• Use your hand sanitizer.

What about constipation? Though I did not, some women experience constipation while on the trail. My best tip: since you will have a different diet on the trail, add more fiber to your diet. You could eat oatmeal every morning. Prunes can be found individually wrapped. And, of course, remember to drink water and stay hydrated all day.

PERIODS

Ah, Aunt Flow, that monthly visitor that is always a pain. Truth is, we have a variety of choices for dealing with our period on a multi-month thru-hike.

Birth Control. Several birth control options allow you to skip your period for several months (or even your whole thru-hike!). Ask your doctor.

Period Cup. A period cup, such as the DivaCup, makes having a period pretty easy. No tampons needed, and you just empty the cup every 12 hours. Research the options, then try them and be comfortable with them *before* you start the AT. Be aware that placement of the cup is different than tampons, and you'll need to have clean hands as well as be able to clean the cup before reinserting each time. There are several different brands available.

Tampons/pads. I guess I'm pretty old-fashioned as I used what I normally do – tampons. However, I did make a couple of changes. I switched to the brand o.b., which have a thin, plastic, outer wrapper and no plastic applicator – all you need is your finger to guide the tampon. These were smaller and lighter to pack and made the least amount of trash for me to carry out. You must not bury your tampons or wrappers on the trail, nor can you leave them in the privies.

The second change I made was to eliminate the overnight pad. No way did I want to deal with pads on the trail. I did some research and reached out to some girlfriends for advice. I switched from a pad at night to a tampon and used just one tampon during the day (so one at night, one during the day). Consult your doctor; this may not be right for you; I'm just telling you what I did. My periods were not that heavy on the trail, and because we went to sleep so early, this worked well for me.

I also had a separate, heavy-duty ziplock bag that I put duct tape over so you couldn't see inside it and deposited my used tampons in this. I know this sounds gross, but you absolutely have to carry them out. You can put a dry tea bag in the ziplock bag to help absorb the odor. I kept this ziplock in my TP kit and would hang in my bear bag (food and other scented items go in this bag to be hung each night to keep bears away from it).

By the way, it has long been a myth that bears are attracted to the scent of a woman while she is on her menstruation cycle, but according to a recent report from Yellowstone National Park, both grizzly and black bears are NOT attracted to this scent. Polar bears might be, but if you see one of those, you're on the wrong trail. To be safe, I recommend putting both clean and used tampons in your bear bag.

The good news. After your first month or so on trail, your period will probably not be as heavy as normal and might not last as long as usual. Also, it might completely disappear for several months at a time! In six months on the AT, I only had three very short and light periods. You may have heard of this happening with professional female athletes. Well, guess what? You will be an elite athlete! Your job is to hike; too bad you won't get paid for it.

PRIVIES

A privy on the Appalachian Trail is an enclosed structure (though sometimes not!) with a small box placed over a hole in the ground where human waste is to be deposited. Privies are mainly located at the shelters along the trail, although some shelters do not have privies, and sometimes (rarely) we would come across a privy on the trail with no shelter.

I can't tell you how many times I've been asked how to prevent germs when using the privies. It's actually pretty hard to do, and the truth is, I didn't even try. You don't have enough excess toilet paper to place around the lid (if there *is* a lid; sometimes it's just a hole cut into a wood plank). Nor do you have easy access to soap and hot water.

My best advice is to look before sitting to make sure no excrement is on the lid (I'm just telling it like it is), and then sit yourself down, use it, and then clean yourself with toilet paper, wet wipes and hand sanitizer. Again, only human waste and toilet paper can go into the privy hole – no tampons, no wet wipes (even if biodegradable), nor wrappers of any kind.

The privies can be very stinky and sometimes infested with spiders, flies or bees. If you don't like the privies, then go in the woods. It can be quite peaceful and even more sanitary, and sometimes quicker than standing in a line of hikers early in the morning or late at night.

SEX

If you thru-hike the trail with a spouse or partner, you will often hear "the trail will make you or break you!" And to a certain extent, this is true. If you don't have a good foundation of friendship and respect for each other beforehand, the trail can break you up. The trail will push you to your limits and will reveal the best and worst qualities of yourselves. On the other hand, if you already have a good thing going, the trail can be the best experience of your life (as it was in my case) and can only strengthen your bond.

For those who start their hike solo, it is possible for an on-trail romance to happen. This shouldn't be too shocking; people who spend a lot of time together with common interests will bond and this bond could take a passionate turn if the sparks are there.

Can I have sex on the AT? Of course you can! Just be discreet like you hopefully would ordinarily (*i.e.,* not in a full shelter or a bunk in a hostel bunkroom).

Where can I have sex on the trail? A lot of places! The truth is sex happens frequently on the trail – in tents, in hammocks, in hotels, in the woods (off the beaten path, one would hope) and in private rooms of hostels. Use your imagination, but as always, be conscientious of others. Be respectful when you are sharing space with others to minimize discomfort and awkward conversations later – and to avoid getting an especially descriptive trail name.

Does not showering for days inhibit having sex? Nope! Not at all. You get surprisingly used to living in the woods and to how you and others smell, so much so that you don't really think about it.

Will the all-day, everyday exercise inhibit my libido?

Nope, just the opposite. Sunsets and I had been married for 22 years when we were on the AT, and honestly, we both experienced a heightened libido and had some of the best sex of our life. Strange, I know. Being outdoors in the best shape of our lives with our endorphins in overdrive from the thrill of accomplishing huge physical challenges every day – it had its effects. Hmm… this may be why Sunsets always requested a private room at hostels.

6. HYGIENE

Taking care of our bodies and hair is a major concern for most women heading out for a long hike. This makes sense – most of us have a routine that includes bathing, shaving our legs and armpits, plucking any unwanted facial hair, blow-drying and styling our hair, and putting on make-up. That's a lot of upkeep if you think about it.

Before I headed out on my trek, I was concerned about my hair and shaving. I am a hairy person, so there was no way I was going to let my leg hair grow and be more ape-like than my male counterparts.

We'll cover all things hair and hygiene related here, and I'll also tell you how I took care of myself on trail.

BATHING

Some hikers pack biodegradable soap. A great brand is Dr. Bronner's, which will work for your body, hair, and even your clothes. Always bathe at least 200 feet away from the water source.

What worked for me was the "wet-wipe bath," which was especially great for my feet. After I got to camp, I'd take off all my clothes in my tent. I'd take a wet wipe (or two or three) and clean my face, armpits, feet, legs, crotch area, and under my breasts. This immediately made me feel 100 times better. If you don't do this for your body, at least do this for your feet. It is essential for healthy hiking feet to clean excess mud, dirt and debris from your feet and then let them air out.

A note about deodorant: don't bother bringing it. You will sweat and stink on the trail whether you use it or not. When I first set out, it was hard for me not to bring deodorant, but I didn't miss it as much as I thought. Yes, I would have enjoyed putting it on after a shower in town, but before I knew it, I was on the trail, hiking again. And when I say hiking, I mean sweating.

I do know a hiker who took a travel-size deodorant with her as her luxury item, and she absolutely loved having it with her because it made her feel better mentally. If this is your case – go for it. You can always toss it in a "hiker box" (a box in trail towns where hikers can leave or take things for free) if you don't want it anymore. Remember, you decide what your final pack weight will be, but the heavier it is, the harder it will be to carry it for five to seven months on the trail.

Makeup. I hope it goes without saying that there is absolutely no need for makeup on the trail. Even if you've worn it every day of your life and it makes you feel better. Trust me that the thru-hiking community is the best place to be yourself and be accepted for your naked face. No one expects you to wear make-up; rather, you will be out of place if you do. Every thru-hiker on the trail has a single focus – to finish the trail within 12 months; how you dress and look goes by the wayside.

I am not one of those natural beauties, but I have never felt more comfortable in my own skin than when I was living in the woods for six months. In fact, after I completed the trail, I literally struggled with styling my hair or applying makeup – it almost felt like I wasn't being true to myself. Every morning BAT (before the AT), I would shower, blow-dry and curl my hair, and apply makeup. AAT (you got it, after the AT), I only shower every other day, air dry my hair, and minimally apply makeup or touch up my hair only if I'm going out and meeting people.

HEAD OF HAIR

Washing your hair or not while in the woods is a personal preference. I chose not to.

When you are in a trail town, most hostels/hotels will have shampoo and soap. Some will have conditioner, but don't count on this. Because I like to be prepared and can't count on others to supply me with toiletries, I carried a tiny travel-size shampoo and an equally small bar of soap, which I shared with Sunsets. I almost never had to use these, but I'm happy I carried them because a few tent sites and shelters on the trail had a shower. A quick shower with soap and shampoo totally refreshed me, but you can get by without packing toiletries. A shower with water only would have been equally refreshing to me – anything to wash off all the sweat and grime.

Different hair types need different care on the trail.

Thick/wavy medium length hair: I have semi-long, thick, wavy hair that typically gets greasy within a day after washing. On my thru-hike, I would braid my hair into two braids and wear my buff as a headband, which covered my greasy roots and also protected my head from the sun. Sometimes I wore a baseball cap. At night I would undo my hair, brush it with a travel-size brush, and let it air out. This actually worked great for me – the longest I went was seven days without a shower and my braids still looked good.

Super long hair: I recommend braiding it – French or regular braids, one braid or two. Braids manage your hair so it doesn't become tangled and are also the best way to keep ticks out. You can do several different kinds of braiding, but French and regular take the least amount of time. You can also wear them in a top-knot bun, which works well with a buff or bandana.

Short hair or shaved head: If you have really short hair or a shaved head, this is the best case scenario for long-distance hiking. Not only is it easy to maintain, but it keeps you cool and allows you to see ticks that may be crawling on you. Easy to wash when in town, easy for everyday hiking, and you don't even need to brush! Some short hair is just long enough to put into pigtails, which keeps it off your neck and is cute to boot – especially with a hat or a buff.

Long, curly hair: I asked a couple of my curly-haired, thru-hiking girlfriends what worked for them. You will hear more from Attie and SwissMiss in Section IV "Conversations with Badass Women Hikers."

Attie: *Braids were a must to keep the tangles at bay. About halfway through the hike, I would French-braid my hair and wear a hat during the day. Once I got to camp, I would let my hair down and take off the hat to let it all air out. Then, I'd re-braid it right before going to bed.*

Also, I actually took trail baths when I was feeling super greasy – would fill up both bottles of water and hike away from the stream. Then, use one bottle to wet my hair, suds up with biodegradable shampoo, then use the second bottle to rinse. This helped me feel refreshed and rejuvenated. I didn't do this on a regular basis, but it was a real pick-me-up when I did.

One more thing, a high bun and a buff worked nicely during the day, too!

SwissMiss: *I would generally pull my hair back in some fashion or braid it. I actually found that not washing my hair for days on end ended up helping my locks because I was not stripping them of precious oils.*

I always brushed and braided my hair at night. Having your hair pulled back for long periods of time can really damage the hair follicle, so braiding was my go-to. It made me look somewhat "put together" and always made me feel pretty.

My routine was to brush my hair in the morning and evening with a wooden brush. Distributing oils with the action of brushing really helped, and although the wooden brush wasn't light, it was my comfort item and it felt HEAVENLY!

My favorite way to wear my hair while hiking is either in a topknot or braids. I often wore a hat which covered up oily roots but still let my braids blow in the wind and look all pretty and shiny (thank you, natural oils).

Because proper hair products are so important for curly hair and conditioner is basically our lifeline, I always made sure to carry my own travel-sized conditioner and shampoo with me (or I would send it to myself in advance if I couldn't get it in stores). It was not realistic to assume that a hostel would have exactly what I needed for my locks.

It felt really luxurious to get to wash and condition my hair with the products I loved in town and it was always something I looked forward to.

Dreadlocks: Here to represent information regarding dreadlocks is Handstand, from whom you'll hear more in Chapter 14.

In some ways, dreadlocks are probably easier to care for on the trail as opposed to brushable hair. You can wash less often, no need to brush it or worry about tangles, and you can even use them to tie your hair up in a ponytail.

However, dreadlocks are not really a temporary style that you would just do for the hike. Depending on your hair texture, they may take a while to form and/or need a lot of maintenance, especially in the early stages, if you want them to look neat and uniform. They also will be difficult to remove after-the-fact, although it is usually possible. I actually create and maintain dreadlocks and dreadlock extensions for work! To find out more about the process, you can visit my website www.lizkidderhair.com.

In my regular life, I wash my hair about once a week. While on trail, I've only been washing it once per month. The most important thing about dreadlocks is keeping them as dry as possible, so the more often they get wet, the better you need to be about blow-drying. Blow-dryers are sometimes hard to come by on the trail or in towns, which is why I have been washing less often. My hair and scalp are used to being washed less often since my hair has been in dreadlocks for so long (eight years), so my scalp doesn't really get dry, itchy or oily, which is great on the trail. Sometimes in the early stages of having dreadlocks, your scalp goes through a transitional phase where those things can happen because it isn't used to being in dreadlocks yet. Like I said earlier, it's nice not to have to worry about doing anything to it in the morning, i.e., brushing, detangling, or braiding. Very easy on the trail!

The downside: When they get wet, they STAY wet for a long time without blow-drying. When I first started the trail in April, I had to be careful about keeping them dry because if they were to get wet, they would stay wet overnight when it got cold, and I would have to worry about hypothermia. Even if it was a light rain, or just really wet or misty out, I would have to be meticulous about wearing a hooded rain jacket and keeping them dry. Once it got warmer, hypothermia was not as much of a concern, but I still wouldn't want to sleep with sopping wet hair, so even if it was too hot for a rain jacket, I would have to wear one anyway.

A lot of people think that it would be hot having them, but I don't think that it is any different than having long hair. If anything, air gets into my scalp easier because it is grouped and separated, instead of a million single strands of hair. I still wear it up in a ponytail or bun like anyone else with long hair when it's really hot out.

BODY HAIR

To shave or not to shave? Many women thru-hikers totally stop shaving – both their armpits and their legs. I admire them greatly. As I said earlier, I am a hairy person, and I was not about to grow the hair out on my legs. Instead, I shaved about once a week whenever we stayed at a hostel for a shower. I did NOT worry about it on the trail during the week. Sure I had some major stubble, but you couldn't tell unless you were sitting right next to me staring at my legs.

If you don't want to shave, don't shave! Another option, if you're self-conscious about it, is to wear short-sleeve shirts and leggings. One of my friends wore leggings every day anyway – she liked the protection from brush, ticks and rock scrambles.

What about facial hair? I took tweezers, an eyebrow razor trimmer, and a small magnifying mirror with me for face grooming. I sometimes tweezed my face at night in my tent, but most of the time I waited until I had a well-lit bathroom in town.

UNDERWEAR

Bras: If you are small enough, go commando. I so wish I could have done this, but being pretty well endowed, I needed some support for my girls. I, as well as most of my friends, highly recommend merino wool for a sports bra. You may have heard of this miraculous material typically used by hikers in socks and shirts. A four-season material, merino wool is not your grandmother's wool – it doesn't itch and it keeps you cool in hot weather and warm in cold weather. It breathes and manages moisture extremely well – it can retain 30% of its own weight in moisture and still feel dry to the touch. It also dries quickly, which is a necessity for thru-hikers. Perhaps best of all, merino wool is odor resistant. Because of the effective moisture-wicking properties, odor-causing bacteria don't have the environment they need to thrive.

I had the Smartwool brand merino wool bra, and it was very comfy. Remember, you don't need 100% support because you're not running and jumping; you are walking.

Mine was so comfortable I sometimes slept in it. Highly recommended.

Underwear: Some women will go commando. If you are comfortable with this, go for it. I wish I could have, but I seem to sweat a lot down there when exercising and felt more comfortable having an extra layer between my shorts and me. I highly recommend the brand ExOfficio Sport Mesh (exofficio.com), and tons of other women swear by this brand as well. The Give-N-Go Sport Mesh style is lightweight, breathable, comfortable, quick-drying, and it comes in many different styles. My favorite is the hipkini – it never creeps up on me.

CHAFING

Chafing can be a painful thing on the trail. I can't believe I had zero issues with this as most thru-hikers (men and women alike) do. Chafing happens when skin constantly rubs against either fabric or skin. The most common areas are thighs and butt cheeks; however, the feet, nipples, armpits, breasts (particularly underneath the breasts), and groin can also chafe. When you are hiking, your skin is hot and sweaty and more likely to chafe. If the chafing is not addressed promptly, it can develop into an infection.

How to prevent chafing: Wear compression shorts or leggings. A tight material hugging (but not rubbing) your thighs will prevent irritating friction, while wearing loose hiking pants can cause chafing because the material moves and rubs against the skin. Products that help prevent chafing include Body Glide, Gold Bond Friction, Lady Monkey Butt, Vaseline, and even deodorant can work in a pinch.

Some women love hiking in a dress or a skirt. If your thighs do not touch each other when you walk, great! But if they do, wearing a thin pair of compression shorts underneath your dress or skirt will help. Make sure they are long enough to cover the parts of your thighs that touch. I love to hike in a skort, but for long-distance hiking, I need to make sure the shorts are long enough to cover my thighs where they touch.

How to recover: The best thing to do is to heal first – that means take at least a day off from hiking. Wash the area carefully with mild soap and pat dry (no rubbing, you've done enough of that already). Apply either Vaseline or Desitin on the area and keep it exposed to the air. If the area is throbbing with pain, you can apply an ice pack for short periods of time.

GLASSES / CONTACTS

Those who wear contacts may want to consider wearing glasses while hiking on the trail. Your hands will always be dirty on the trail, and they need to be clean to put in your contacts. Of course, you can clean your hands, but it may simply be easier to wear glasses and take them off to sleep. If you do wear glasses, make sure the fit is snug without being too tight; you don't want them to slip down your nose when you sweat. Also, be aware that they will fog up in the rain.

I knew women who wore their contacts on the trail; it was worth it to them to go through the trouble of carrying the solution. Other options are extended wear lenses and disposable lenses. Do your research and find out what will work best for you. Make sure you have a plan for cleaning your hands sufficiently before inserting or removing your contacts.

FOOT CARE

Toenails: Keeping toenails clipped as short as possible is important. Clip straight across the top, not a rounded cut. I filed my toenails after I cut them to smooth any edges out so they wouldn't snag on my socks. If your toenails are long, even if your shoes fit properly, your nails can press into the tip of your shoe causing you pain, blisters, and possible bleeding. Remember, you are not walking on a level path all day; your hike is more like an obstacle course. The longer your toenails, the more likely they will be crushed against the shoes as you walk, especially while hiking a steep decline.

Hot spots: A hot spot is an area of skin that feels hot or excessively rubbed. As soon as you feel this anywhere on your feet – stop. A hot spot is a warning that a blister is about to form, but you still have time to keep it from fully forming. Apply Leukotape, moleskin, or your preferred sports tape. The tape acts as a barrier between your skin and socks to stop the friction.

Blisters: What do you do if a blister has already formed? The first coarse of action is to cut a blister-size hole in a piece of moleskin or foam, place over the blister and attach it with Leukotape or duct tape. This will protect the blister and evade further friction. Avoid draining if possible and dress it like a wound if it pops.

KT Tape is a magical tape that can be stretched tight over a troublesome muscle or sore area to keep the area sturdy (as if you wrapped it in an Ace bandage). Numerous videos on YouTube demonstrate wrapping different kinds of aches or injuries. I used KT Tape all the time on my hike – for my knees, ankles, and feet. Something somewhere was always bothering me.

Swollen feet: Thru-hikers' feet will swell during the day – big surprise, right? You are hiking on them for most of the day, and besides your body weight, you also have your pack weight to consider. Your poor feet! The swelling doesn't hurt, unless your shoes don't have room to allow for this. One thing I did in my tent at the end of the day was to prop my feet up on my backpack. This helped to reduce the swelling, and it also just felt good.

What's in Chica's hygiene kit?

- *Small magnifying mirror*
- *Tweezers (for eyebrows, stray hairs, or ticks)*
- *Noxzema eyebrow shaver (for when tweezers are not enough)*
- *Fingernail clippers and file*
- *Hairbrush and rubber bands*
- *Wet wipes*

- *Vitamin I (Ibuprofen)*
- *Leukotape*
- *Bandages and Neosporin*

7. WILDLIFE

Living in the woods for days on end, you are bound to come into contact with wildlife; after all, this is their home. The information below, along with your own research, will help you be prepared for these animals.

TICKS

A tiny creature that is sometimes barely visible to the naked eye, the tick should be your biggest concern on the trail. While Lyme disease, transmitted by the deer tick (aka black-legged tick), is the most common tick-borne disease, each variety of tick can transmit multiple illnesses, including Rocky Mountain spotted fever, carried by the wood tick, and southern tick-associated rash illness from the lone star tick. Ticks are located all along the trail and often get picked up by the hiker in tall grass.

Ticks that have been attached for less than 24 hours are unlikely to have infected you with Lyme or any other disease. Daily tick checks can help spot climbers and those that may have attached. Keep in mind that the deer tick, the main culprit of Lyme disease, is the size of a poppy seed in the nymph stage and can be hard to spot.

Tip: Have your clothes treated with permetherin. Besides ticks, permethrin also helps prevent against mosquitos, flies, ants, chiggers, midges and fleas. You can treat your clothes with permetherin yourself, but this is only good for seven washings, so you will need to repeat it throughout your hike. We sent our clothes to a company called Insect Shield. They professionally treated our clothing with permetherin, which is good for 70 washings (will last a whole thru-hike). Also, check for ticks every night as we talked about earlier.

SNAKES

Know what kinds of snakes are on the AT, which ones are poisonous, and what they look like. Know what to do when you see one in the middle of the trail. Be on the lookout for them especially when climbing over rocks and boulders. My eyes were always glued to the ground anyway to prevent myself from tripping, but I still missed snakes! My husband and I saw a total of 37 snakes on our hike due to the fact that Sunsets, a snake-whisperer who loves snakes, was constantly on the lookout for them. I would walk right by them all the time – twice I even stepped right over a snake – and he often called me back to see what I had missed.

Several types of snakes can be found along the 2,200 miles of the Appalachian Trail, but only three are venomous. Always look at the head of the snake for a triangular shape which usually denotes that the snake is venomous. Here are the three venomous types:

The **timber rattlesnake** will usually make its presence known with a distinctive shake (rattle), but almost as often, it will lie stealthily silent, sometimes in the middle of the trail, sometimes in the tall grass parallel to the trail. This snake can be seen in almost any state along the AT.

The **copperhead** is most likely to be encountered along the trail from Georgia to New York. The name describes how it looks – the head is the color of a copper penny, and the patterned color is its most distinguishing feature.

The **cottonmouth or water moccasin** is infrequently seen on the trail (in fact, you'll probably never see one). They are only found in the first 20 miles of the AT starting at the southern terminus in Georgia. They prefer lower elevations and water.

What if a snake bites me? According to the CDC (cdc.gov), "It has been estimated that 7,000-8,000 people per year receive venomous bites in the United States, and about five of those people die." So it is highly unlikely you will be bitten in the first place, and even more doubtful that you will die if bitten. On the rare chance that you are bitten by a venomous snake, you will need antivenin – the faster the better.

*What **not** to do:* Evidence suggests snakebite kits are ineffective and could even make the situation more dangerous. Do not buy or bring one. Forget everything you have seen in movies when someone is bitten. Do not cut an "X" around the bite with your knife. Do not try to suck the venom, and don't apply a tourniquet.

*What you **should** do:* The first step is to stay calm (ha!), walk a good distance from the snake, and sit down. Remove any tight-fitting jewelry or clothing from the bite area as it is going to swell. Call 911 if you have a cell signal. Use a pen or sharpie to mark the edge of swollen areas every 15 minutes; this can help medical personnel determine the extent of envenomation. And finally, hike to the nearest road, preferably with another hiker, and get to a hospital as quickly as possible.

Tips: The most obvious advice is to stay far away from any snakes you see, venomous or not. If they are in the middle of the trail, walk off the trail to go around them. If you can't go around them (sometimes the woods and brush are dense on either side of the trail or there may be a severe drop-off), try to get them to move by throwing sticks or rocks near them. Do not use your trekking poles as this will put you too close to the snake. Snakes usually hang out in rocks and woodpiles, so always pay attention to where you place your hands when rock scrambling or gathering wood.

BEARS

The American black bear is the only type of bear found on the length of the Appalachian Trail. Black bears like human food, and this is evident in their high population near national and state parks, where humans hang out in high numbers and are sometimes not well versed in hanging or storing their food out of the reach of bears. Bears that have become accustomed to interacting with humans lose their fear of them and often become a nuisance.

Hikers are strongly encouraged to store their food properly with bear cables, on a bear pole, or in bear boxes, any of which may be found at some shelters. If none of these are available, you must hang a bear bag in a tree or use a bear canister.

You may see a bear anywhere along the AT, but they are most prominently found in Shenandoah National Park, New Jersey, and the Great Smoky Mountains National Park. A good practice is to whistle, talk, or sing to let bears know you are in the area and so you don't startle them.

What should I do if I see a bear? Don't run and don't make eye contact. Never drop food to distract or appease the bear. If the bear has not seen you, you should slowly retreat from the bear. If it has seen you, make yourself known by talking calmly and assertively to the bear; the subject matter is inconsequential. Most likely it will move on about its business.

If it seems interested in you and doesn't move on, make yourself appear as large as possible. Raise trekking poles with your arms high above your head and yell loudly at the bear. Black bears may stand on their hind legs, swat their paws at the ground, or even make a bluff charge whereby they run towards you but stop short of a maul. These are all opportunities for you to calmly (yeah, right) back away from the situation. Always make sure the bear has a way out as well – don't block its only path.

It is VERY rare, but if the encounter escalates into an attack, you need to fight back and fight dirty. If you have bear spray, use it. Use your trekking poles. Pummel its snout with your fists and gouge its eyes with your fingers. Unlike with grizzly bears, playing dead does not work. You must fight. Oh, and black bears are faster than you could ever be, at both running and climbing trees. Sorry.

Much to Sunsets' dismay, I carried a mini air horn with me when we started our trek. I was worried about seeing a bear, even though I knew it would probably want nothing to do with me. I never used the air horn and ended up putting it in a hiker box at some point. We saw only four bears on our hike, all of them only half-grown, and all ran away from us as soon as they saw us. I was actually disappointed that none of them were close enough for me to get a picture.

PORCUPINES

There are more than two dozen species of porcupines, but you will only encounter the North American porcupine along the Appalachian Trail. Porcupines love salt, and guess what? A thru-hiker sweats a lot and is therefore very salty. Porcupines will frequent shelters as they like to gnaw on the salt-encrusted edge of the platform floor – exactly where hikers tend to sit and congregate with their salty legs hanging over the edge.

A porcupine has quills that lie flat against their outer body until they are threatened and they stand to attention as a deterrent to other predators. Porcupines cannot shoot their quills as once thought, but they will detach very easily if touched. So stay far away from them, and certainly don't touch them!

If you encounter a porcupine, give them space and time to wander away or give them a wide berth if you decide to walk around them. They may be stubborn and slow to move.

MICE

The rodents most hikers are concerned with are those that share shelter space with the hikers – mice and chipmunks. You may have heard horror stories of a mouse running across a hiker's face in a shelter in the middle of the night. Yep, it can happen.

Although they are always drawn to crumbs left by sloppy hikers, mice also love backpacking gear and will often gnaw on bags, bandanas, and backpacks to acquire nesting material. When in shelters, always use the provided mouse hanger (a hanging cord with a tin can to block mice and a stick attached to hang backpacks).

Tip: A wise hiker unzips all of her backpack pockets, particularly the hip belt pockets. If a mouse does get to your bag, you want to give it easy access rather than having it burrow a hole in your gear. We heard of mice gnawing their way into a backpack pocket, even though no food was left, because the scent still lingered.

Because I didn't want to hear mice running around the shelter (or, god forbid, feel them running over my face), and because we liked our privacy, we opted to tent out almost every night. We did sleep in a shelter twice; after all, I wanted to have "the full thru-hiking experience" (Sunsets cringed whenever I said that). I did not see, hear, or feel any mice either time.

MOSQUITOS / BLACK FLIES

Mosquitos can be anywhere on the trail but are most prominent in the summer. I had a separate insect head-net for this purpose ($2 at Walmart) which worked great. A tip for bug nets – wear a hat with a brim under the net to keep it from touching your face. The first time I tried the bug net with no hat, I found it much more annoying than you'd think to have it touching my face.

Besides my clothing being treated with permethrin, I also used an insect spray (Deep Woods OFF!), which worked sufficiently against the mosquitoes. There are several other products you can use as well.

The black flies in Maine can be a real problem, but luckily, by the time I arrived at the end of August, the weather had cooled and they were completely gone.

MOOSE

You will know you're in moose country when you start seeing mounds of moose-poop pellets along the trail. They are most prevalent in Maine, New Hampshire, Vermont, and even some parts of Massachusetts. Moose can be unpredictable and aggressive. If you see them, give them time to move along. If a moose becomes aggressive, put yourself in a position so that a large solid tree or similar structure is between you and the moose. It is unlikely you will be attacked by a moose; in fact, it's highly probable that you won't even see one.

MEN

Ah yes, that mysterious and rare breed of animal. In all seriousness, one might feel as if they are a different species sometimes. While I certainly met many women on the trail, I met even more men. I have to say, I loved hanging out and being one of the guys. Virtually all of the guys I met on the trail were cool and treated me respectfully; they were polite, down to earth, and easy to talk to and to get along with. You may think this was because I was hiking with my husband, but we were not always together.

I talk in Chapter 2 about the possibility of guys who are jerks or who give off creepy vibes, but remember, most of the men you meet on the trail will be great guys.

III: EVERYTHING IN BETWEEN

"Adventure is worthwhile in itself."

– AMELIA EARHART

This section includes other stuff about thru-hiking that is not necessarily related to fears or worries, but is just darn good information to know – no matter what your sex is.

JEN BECK SEYMOUR

8. MAKING CONNECTIONS

I am amazed that I can do all the research in the world, but sometimes I just don't get the full picture until I talk to someone about it. Even if they haven't been to the place I'm researching, they may ask a question or make a comment that offers me a perspective I hadn't considered.

So how do you connect with people to further your quest for information, encouragement, and even practical help while on the trail?

GO TELL IT ON THE MOUNTAIN

Telling your family and friends about your forthcoming epic journey is a huge deal. By verbalizing the decision aloud, you are solidifying the plan for yourself as well. Of course, I recommend telling them *after* you have already completed your research, formulated a plan, and committed to your thru-hike.

Get ready for some shocked and incredulous looks. We talked about this earlier. Remember to give them time to soak it in, be patient, and be prepared to answer questions. As they learn from you, they may aid your determination with their encouragement. Don't let negative people deter you. Show them you know what you're doing by answering their questions calmly and positively.

We did not know until after we finished that a few of Sunsets' and my own brothers(!) didn't think we would make it all the way. A couple in New Hampshire, who had watched our videos from the beginning, graciously invited us into their home for trail magic and told us that they had not believed we would get far past Day One. Of course, they had changed their tune by the time we arrived in New Hampshire.

Building a support system at home is important, particularly if you have someone who can send you different gear when the weather changes and who is home to receive gear that you no longer need.

If you're lucky, you may have some friends and family offer to send you care packages along the way. Planning this is a bit difficult. My advice is to ask if you can contact them about one to two weeks out when you are ready to give them an address for sending it. Another good idea is to give them a list of things you will want or need instead of making them guess and having too much food left over.

SOCIAL MEDIA

I am an introvert, but that doesn't mean I don't like people, especially people with whom I have a connection or who share common interests, such as thru-hiking the Appalachian Trail.

Of course, the support of family and friends is great, but you can benefit greatly from the experience of people who have already hiked the AT. Even those who are planning to walk may share some excellent resources with you and could likewise benefit from your research.

Granted, not everyone is interested in thru-hiking the Appalachian Trail, so if you don't already have AT connections, here are a few places to start:

• **Instagram** is great because you can search by hash tags (#appalachiantrail #appalachiantrailthruhike #AT2020, *etc.*) and find people to follow. You never know what you might learn from someone in the same place as you – in the planning stages for an AT thru-hike.

• **YouTube:** YouTube.com is a tool I used frequently, starting in 2015. Watching various vlogs about AT thru-hikes has several benefits. You can literally see the trail and how hard it can be. You can see some of the trail towns and landmarks (it was so cool finally to be there and to recognize these familiar places in person!). You can also see what gear other hikers are currently using, and sometimes they'll talk about it or what doesn't work for them and why. Watching gear list videos made both before and after the vlogger's thru-hike is quite beneficial. And people who quit often make a final video about it; I found these to be invaluable. This is where my "power of negative thinking" comes in – if you know ahead of time what factors make people quit, you can deal with it better when it happens to you.

• **TrailJournals.com:** This is a free website devoted to people planning for and hiking trails (not just the AT). You can search for people to follow and also write your own journals about your trek. This website is particularly useful for people who want to journal about their trip but don't have their own website or blog.

Of course, you could always write the old fashioned way too – in a real paper journal. I did a little bit of everything – a small paper notebook, short daily posts on Facebook and

Instagram, and daily vlogs on YouTube. The paper notebook has come in handy since my hike: I can easily look back on a date and see where I was, how many miles I hiked, what happened and what I felt. I also referred to it with helping put together a Shutterfly photo book of our AT adventure.

• **Facebook groups:** One of the benefits of my ultra-organized mindset is that I like to plan and research everything. In my research of the Appalachian Trail, I came across several Facebook groups.

You can find a surplus of Appalachian Trail Facebook groups; however, I am only recommending two of them since most of the groups have too many "armchair hikers" – people who haven't set foot on the trail yet (or in a long time) but still love to give advice, usually highly-opinionated advice. Other times you will encounter inexplicably mean, negative people, who like dragging others down. Of course, you can eventually weed out the trolls and Debbie Downers, but if you are a newbie to these groups, the negativity could discourage you and I don't want that to happen to you.

The first group I recommend is *Appalachian Trail Class of 20_ _* (whatever year you will be hiking the AT). This will give you a smaller group, and you'll all be going the same year, so you will have much in common and hopefully will meet each other on the trail as well.

The second group I recommend is *Appalachian Trail: Women's Group*. Whether you are planning a section-, long-distance, day- or thru-hike of the Appalachian Trail, you will find like-minded women who only want to support one another in this amazing, drama-free atmosphere. You can ask anything and the tribe of women will offer up their advice honestly and positively. The last thing you need to worry about is feeling stupid or weird about asking questions. No topic is off limits, as long as it has to do with women hiking the Appalachian Trail.

I made some wonderful friends in the women's group before I started my hike, and then I met some of them in person while I was on my thru-hike. Two women in particular helped me tremendously.

Moo Bear and I connected way before our 2017 thru-hike as we both had Morton's neuroma issues with our feet. I had never heard of Morton's neuroma and had never had painful foot issues before, so I went to a doctor and fortunately did not have a severe case; rest from hiking, orthopedic inserts, and exercises eventually did the trick for me. However, I was freaking out because we were supposed to start in a few months and here I was – limping! More than anything, it helped to talk to someone who was going through the same odd thing – she was further in the recovery stage and encouraged me through my fears and concerns. Thankfully, we both felt fine by the time we started our thru-hike attempt, and neither of us had any return issues with Morton's neuroma again.

I knew **Karma** from the women's group as well (she had bought some of the jewelry I make). About one week before we left for the trail, Sunsets and I took a six-mile hike in the snow-packed woods of Wisconsin with our full packs. By that time, I had had my Osprey Exos 48L pack for almost a year and had been hiking with it in Costa Rica and Wisconsin. Looking back, I had ongoing concerns with it, but because it was very lightweight, I *wanted* to love it so badly that I often ignored the issues. After this particular hike, I was seriously hurting. I had experienced hip pain before, but never this severe, and it would usually clear up in a day or two. This time I could not ignore it. It had to be the pack. The Exos is a great pack, but it is unisex, so not specifically made for a woman, and its super-light weight means no extra padding on it anywhere. Great time to acknowledge my problem, huh? We were far away from the closest outfitter, and even if I ordered a new pack, I had no time to practice and make sure it was a better fit. What to do?

Enter the women's group. I posted on the group page about my problem and stress. Karma sent me a personal message almost immediately. Even as I type this, I still can't believe what happened. She was thru-hiking too, AND would be staying at Amicalola Lodge (near the GA start) the same time I was, AND just happened to have an extra backpack! This was not just any pack – it was the Osprey Aura 50L AG. I had read great reviews of this pack, and actually had my eye on it. Though quite a bit heavier than the Exos, it was specifically made for a woman with continuous padding around the back and hips (no seams for rubbing). The front hip belt was adjustable and you could lengthen or shorten the padded part. The torso was fully adjustable.

She offered to bring her extra backpack to Amicalola with her (she was driving and had room). I could try it on in my hotel room, pack it up with my gear, adjust all the bells and whistles, and see what I thought. Of course, I wouldn't be able to practice with it, but she had a solution for that too. I could send the Exos ahead on the trail to our first stop at Neel's Gap and wear the Aura at the start of our trek. If it wasn't a good fit, I'd only have to deal with it for four to five days and then could switch back to the Exos (and send the Aura back to her home address). And if it did work out (which it did!), I could send the Exos back to my home address (which I did!).

They say the trail provides, and it does, but it's also good to have a bit of good karma. Karma probably saved my thru-hike experience and maybe my sanity as well! She offered me a solution and swept away all my fears and concerns.

My Osprey Aura 50L

When Greg and I connected with our class on Facebook, we got to know another couple our age, and we soon discovered we were all starting around the same day in March. We found them at Amicalola Lodge and were able to say "hi" to them in person before we started. We never saw them again, but we followed each other on social media and shared advice, which worked out great for all of us.

That leads me to another point: when you meet other hikers for the first time on the trail, even if you never see them again, following each other on social media (particularly Facebook and Instagram) is not a bad idea. Whoever is ahead can give tips and advice to whomever is behind. This works great in case of wildfires that might be burning, trail closures, viruses at certain water sources, good hostels or hotels, places where "you just have to eat" or AYCE (all-you-can-eat) buffets, *etc.* And don't forget to pass on information to the people following you as well.

Because we posted on Facebook, Instagram and YouTube in real time during our thru-hike, we received several offers from trail angels. (You need to be able to trust your gut instincts – if someone seems a little off, don't accept their offer.) We were fortunate enough to make friends with some wonderful people who either welcomed us into their homes, gave us rides, or provided some other trail magic. I was continually overwhelmed by the amazing people who wanted to meet and help us!

9. BUDGETING

I cannot emphasize enough how important it is to research and budget for your hike. Two of the most critical needs – time and money – are exactly what no one ever seems to have enough of.

TIME

Long-distance walking on a whim seems to be a trend these days. If Sunsets had his way, he would've set foot on the trail the day after he decided he wanted to do it! Okay, that's one way to do it – but if your goal is not only to start but also to finish a thru-hike, you need that precious commodity we call time. Giving yourself enough time to prepare for and to complete this epic challenge can save you money and frustration and will give you the best chance of reaching your goal.

TIME BEFORE THE TRAIL

Sunsets and I had made the decision to thru-hike the AT a year and a half in advance of starting out. We were living in Costa Rica at the time, and though we loved our time there, after four years, we were ready for the next adventure. The Appalachian Trail fit the bill. Luckily, we lived in the Central Valley – the perfect training ground for the AT – where we hiked up and down mountains every morning.

In addition to giving us time to transition from living in a foreign country, this year and a half also gave us patience to wait for the gear we wanted to go on sale. Hiking gear, especially lightweight gear that is durable enough to withstand six months of abuse, is expensive. By having time and shopping wisely, we were able to cut our gear costs by about 45%.

This period before the trail also gave us time to research and make connections on social media (see Chapter 8).

TIME ON THE TRAIL

While taking enough time to plan your hike is important, giving yourself enough time to complete the hike is just as critical.

How do I estimate how much time I need for my thru? It's mostly a guessing game, but here are some rough parameters for estimating.

You'll need to pick a number of miles that you think you will hike per day once you get your trail legs. Say that number is 16 miles a day. Take the total number of miles on the Appalachian Trail (it changes every year; let's estimate it at 2,190), and divide by your daily estimated miles.

2,190 / 16 = 137 days (or 19.5 weeks)

Then add in a zero day once a week, or however often you think you might need one.

137 + 19 zeros = 156 days

That is a VERY rough estimate. Keep in mind you should start with slower miles in the beginning, to give your body time to ease into its new routine. Also when you get to the Whites in New Hampshire, your mileage may decrease (ours did!).

The majority of AT thru-hikers take five to seven months. We calculated conservatively we would take six months but scheduled enough time and money for seven months' hiking. Even though we had some sections where we took a few more zeros than planned, we finished our thru just one day shy of six months.

MONEY

Unless you have a map to all the money trees along the AT, you will need a budget for your hike. There are two ways to budget finances for a hike:

1. Know what kind of hike you want to take (tight-budget? middle-of-the-road? luxurious?) and save enough money for the specific needs you will encounter.

2. Start with whatever amount of money you already have at your disposal, and plan for the type of hike this money allows.

We chose option number one with a middle-of-the-road budget as we had time to save the money we thought we'd need. I do not recommend option two as your total amount may not allow for the time you need on the trail and also may not allow for emergencies (illness, injury, extra zero days, gear repairs, *etc.*).

You might be shocked at how much it costs to wander around in the woods for half a year. Everyone has their own view of the type of hike they would like to have; however, generally speaking, most thru-hikers spend $2 - $3 per mile while on trail or about $1000 a month, more or less. This budget includes food while on the trail, hostel or hotel stays while in town, gear repair or replacement, injuries, illnesses and other on-trail costs.

Other expenses to consider are your initial cost of gear, travel to and from the terminuses, and at-home costs while you are away. Gear can be expensive and is necessary to keep you safe and relatively comfortable. Depending on what gear you already have, equipping a thru-hike can cost from $1500 to over $3000. You will also need transportation to and from the trail. Both Springer Mountain and Mount Katahdin are remote, and in addition to flying or busing into a nearby city, you will need to arrange for a shuttle and probably a hostel or hotel stay. Don't forget your ongoing expenses at home, which you need to take care of while on trail (rent, mortgage, car and health insurance, cell phone bills, *etc.*).

Finally, remember what it is you are doing – hiking in rough terrain in inclement weather. Your body and gear are going to suffer. Money should be set aside for gear repair or replacement, doctor visits and extra hotel stays should you become ill or injured.

Sunsets and I budgeted about $2.50 per person, per mile, and we ended up spending $2.90 per person, per mile. This was fine with us because we had extra money set aside for emergencies and special circumstances. Little did we know that those circumstances would entail an eight-day slack-packing stint in southern Maine and some extra zero days to avoid hiking in snowstorms. The slack-packing gave us the extra mental boost we needed towards the end; I was coming down with a cold and we were both getting physically and mentally tired. A lighter pack and a shower and bed every night gave us that extra push we needed to hike on to Katahdin.

SAVING MONEY ON TRAIL

For the money-conscious hiker, I have a few tips for you on how to save money during your thru-hike.

• Instead of withdrawing cash at ATMs, use your debit card at the grocery store to pay for your supplies, and while you are paying, withdraw whatever cash you need. No ATM fees.

• Some stores have reward cards. Ask politely if you can use the clerk's (you'd be surprised at what a great conversation starter "I'm hiking the Appalachian Trail" is). You can also get your own card before you start the trail or at the first store you encounter with reward cards.

• Always ask for a cash discount at hostels and hotels. One time, we got 20% off! Also, the more people you have, the better the discount you can get for shuttles and slack-packing.

• Do a "nero" (one night stay, fewer meals out) instead of a "zero" (two nights stay, more meals in town, more alcohol, *etc.*).

• Work for stay – you can always ask a hostel owner about "work for stay," which means you work for them instead of paying them. You will do whatever odd jobs the owner wants or needs. Work for stay is also possible in the "huts" in the White Mountains of New Hampshire – huts are scattered along the Whites, mainly for day hikers to stay overnight (they are a bit pricey for most thru-hikers, though anyone can reserve them). Work for stay is only possible on a limited basis, so ask at each hut when you arrive.

• If you drink alcohol, try to buy it at the store and drink it at your hotel or hostel if it is allowed; it's much more affordable this way than buying it at a restaurant. You can also go in with other hikers and split a six-pack of beer or a bottle of wine. Many hotels and hostels have a microwave and a refrigerator – use these instead of going out for every meal.

• Instead of staying in a hostel or hotel, stay at a campsite just outside of town or tent in town for a minimal price. You can't do this in all towns, but check your guidebook for availability. Use the laundry, shower, and resupply services in town, but sleep in your tent for free!

• Split a hotel room. Three to four hikers (and sometimes only two) in a hotel room is almost always cheaper than a hostel, and you'll get more privacy than in a bunk room.

On the list of reasons why prospective thru-hikers quit, after injury, running out of money is at the top of the list. Being financially prepared is imperative for this trip of a lifetime.

Note: Sunsets vlogged about our budget once a week on our thru-hike. You can find his videos (particularly his last video which has all the totals) on our YouTube channel *Chica and Sunsets*.

10. GEAR

Just a decade ago, you would be hard pressed to find gear made specifically for women. However, with more women hiking each year, the demand for women-specific gear is increasing, particularly for backpacks, sleeping bags, air mattresses and hiking shoes. Not only are women's bodies shaped differently from men, but they also regulate temperature differently.

What gear do you need for a thru-hike on the Appalachian Trail? Let's start with the Big Three (the heaviest, most expensive, and most important pieces of gear you will have): shelter, backpack and sleep system. Then, we will cover all the remaining gear. The gear listed in this chapter is all-inclusive for men and women, though I will point out women-specific gear when it is an option.

SHELTER (BIG #1)

You can use any of the five following types of shelter on your thru-hike (or a combination). To help you, I've listed the pros and cons of each.

TENT SHELTERS

I shared a tent with my husband – the Big Agnes Copper Spur 3 – which can fit three people if you don't mind sleeping right next to someone. For the two of us, it was perfect because we had space between us, space on either side, and room above our heads and below our feet when we were lying down. With a door and vestibule on each side, we didn't have to crawl over each other to get in or out. Sturdy enough to hold up for our whole thru-hike (except when a tree branch fell on us in a storm), the Big Agnes was also double-walled, so it never got wet inside.

Pros: Modern tents are relatively easy to set up and you should be able to find tent spots all along the AT. Tents provide durable shelter in wind, rain, and snow while also providing a layer of protection from bugs and animals. They trap heat inside to keep you warm on cold nights. If you hike with a partner, you can share the weight of the tent, or you can select a tent that uses trekking poles as tent poles to limit the extra weight.

Cons: Tents are the heaviest option for a shelter; if you are hiking alone, you will have to take this extra weight into consideration. Tents can be expensive, especially depending on the options you choose. Sometimes it can be difficult to find a perfectly flat spot – roots and rocks can make it uncomfortable even with an air mattress. When the ground is not level, nothing is more annoying than continually rolling into your partner or tent wall.

Two options to consider are double-walled or single-walled tents. Single-walled will be lighter but also will have much more condensation, so you will need to wipe inside the walls every so often to prevent drips from falling on you. Double-walled tents have an outside rain fly and an inside fine-mesh screen. The screen layer alone is great on those clear, pleasant evenings when no rain is in the forecast; you can get much more air flow this way and gaze up at the stars from your bed. The double-wall feature also controls condensation better because you have an extra layer (the mesh screen) between you and the rain fly.

Most hikers will do fine with a three-season tent; however, if you are a southbound hiker, consider the heavier four-season tent.

HAMMOCK

Sleeping in a hammock is like sleeping in a cocoon, one that sways in the wind. Hammock users swear by their hammocks, and I always wanted to try one, but as a couple we wanted to sleep together – not possible in a hammock.

Pros: The most popular feature of the hammock is its comfort. Hikers who have previously slept in a tent say a hammock is much more comfortable. Imagine sleeping on the flat, hard ground in a tent vs. a soft hammock hanging, practically floating, in the air … you get the idea. Prices and weight can be comparable to tents.

Cons: A hammock can quickly lose its charm in heavy wind and rain. Sometimes it is hard to find two sturdy trees the right distance apart. Besides the hammock itself, you will also need a bug bivy (netting that goes over the top to keep out bugs), a tarp to keep out rain, and an under-quilt that goes beneath your hammock in cold weather to protect you from the cold draft.

TARP

A tarp is a large piece of waterproof material. It will not completely contain you. You will be open to the elements on some sides – wind, bugs, *etc.* Many ultralight hikers choose the tarp because of its weight and versatility.

Pros: A tarp's best asset is its weight – virtually nothing, depending on what type of tarp you get. If you are worried about bugs or insects, you can easily use a bug bivy (a mesh enclosure for keeping out insects) underneath the tarp.

Cons: A tarp can take some time to get used to setting it up and might not protect you from the elements as effectively as you'd like.

A friend of ours used a tarp along with a bug bivy on his 2018 hike, and it worked extremely well for him. You can find his videos on YouTube under *Evan's Backpacking Videos.* He spent a long time learning about his tarp and sleep set-up before his hike, and he takes the time in his videos to point out exactly how he sets his tarp each night for the different weather he anticipates.

SHELTER BLAZING and COWBOY CAMPING

Some hikers carry neither tent, hammock, nor tarp. They plan their days to end at a shelter each night, literally hiking from shelter to shelter. On clear nights, they may "cowboy camp" (using only a sleeping bag, open to the elements and the sky above).

Pros: You have absolutely no shelter weight to carry. Shelter blazing and cowboy camping save time with no tent or hammock to set up.

Cons of shelters: You'll have to plan your hike going from shelter to shelter. Because mileage varies between shelters, it may not match your goal for how many miles you want to hike that day. In inclement weather and when hiking in a "bubble" (a large group of hikers that congregate at certain times in certain areas), shelter space may be scarce. You'll also need to be prepared for the shelter culture; smoking and chatter can sometimes be loud and go late into the night.

Cons of cowboy camping: Cowboy camping can be miserable in inclement weather (cold or rain or snow). Also, it's possible that bugs or – god forbid – a snake could curl up next to you.

BACKPACK (BIG #2)

You will currently find women-specific backpacks on the market for virtually any sport – hiking, running, biking, mountain climbing, *etc.* Generally, the differences in women's packs vs. men's packs include a shorter torso, curved shoulder straps to account for our breasts, adjustable hip belts and extra padding on the hip belt.

Your backpack will carry everything you need to live for five to seven months on the Appalachian Trail. Think about that. Some of us live in big houses and have so many tools and toys that we use on a daily basis, but when it comes down to it – all you need to survive on the AT fits into a pack that you carry on your back!

I had the Osprey Aura 50 pack, which I loved. The number in the pack name tells you how many liters it will carry. The Aura 50 is specifically made for a woman: it has an adjustable torso length, comfortable padding inside the hip belt and shoulder straps, and an adjustable hip belt, which came in handy when I started losing weight. I loved all the adjustments that made it fit my body perfectly. Most of the time, I felt like I wasn't even wearing a pack, even though it weighed 27-28 pounds with food and water.

One option on a pack is the frame. Old-school packs all had outer frames that were heavy and rigid and are hardly used any more except for carrying a very heavy weight. Most packs now have an internal frame, but you can also find some completely without a frame (usually the ultralight ones). Keep in mind that a frame will help distribute the weight, and if you are going with a frameless pack, you need to know what it feels like and to be prepared for it. Also, be aware: once you go over the weight maximum on the lightweight packs (even a little), you may develop problems in your back, shoulders, and neck.

If you've never been fitted for a pack, go to a reputable outdoor store and be fitted properly, even if you are not yet ready to buy a pack. The load of your pack should be carried in your hips with only a small percentage of weight on your shoulders. To avoid back, shoulder, and neck pain, you need to know how to properly balance the load so too much weight doesn't ride on your shoulders.

What features do you want in your backpack?

Adjustability. Look for this on the hip belt and torso.

Straps. Some manufacturers (*e.g.,* ULA Equipment) have specific straps – called S straps – that are curved to accommodate women's breasts.

Padding. Look for padding on the top shoulder straps and hips. Men's packs often have only slight padding on the hip belt, sometimes with bothersome seams. My hips needed the seamless, extra padding found on women's packs.

Ventilation. Some packs have a great mesh layer that actually raises the pack off your back (which is where you will likely sweat the most) and allows the sweat to evaporate. My pack had this and I loved it.

Water bladder/hydration reservoir. Some people like to drink from a water bladder. If this is you, make sure your pack has a place for your bladder in the back.

Number of liters. You will most likely need a 45-65 L pack for the AT unless you're going ultralight or you're carrying much more equipment than most.

For brand names of women-specific backpacks, I highly recommend checking out www.OutdoorGearLab.com. They have tested and rated tons of women-specific gear from backpacks and clothing to air mattresses and sleeping bags.

SLEEP SYSTEM (BIG #3)

You will find both sleeping bags and air mattresses specifically made for women. They are made smaller to fit a woman's body better and have more insulation where we need it most (specifically the torso and foot areas).

SLEEPING BAG/QUILT

I used the Enlightened Equipment Revelation 10° bag. Though I am 5'6" tall, I still bought the long size, which worked great for pulling up and over my head on cold nights. Most people are familiar with the regular sleeping bags or mummy bags, but the quilt version is different in that it does not fully attach in the back. When you lie in a sleeping bag, the material under you gets compacted and doesn't keep you warm, so why not eliminate it and make it lighter?

The Revelation has a toe box area that you can cinch shut and zip around your lower legs and feet. Straps attach the quilt to your air mattress, so when you toss and turn at night, the quilt does not move with you. I kept this bag with me the whole trip. In the summer, you can undo the foot box so it is one piece (a quilt!) – very easy to toss off when you get hot or to pull over you when chilled. I loved it and it worked great for me, but it is not for everyone.

Some hikers use one sleeping bag or quilt for their whole thru-hike, while others switch, using one for winter and a lighter one for summer.

What features should you look for in a sleeping bag or quilt?

Degree rating. This is the lowest temperature at which you can "survive," not the temperature at which you will be comfy and warm. For instance, mine had a rating of 10° Fahrenheit, which meant I would need to wear several layers under my quilt to be comfortable at this temperature. I may not be comfortable, but I wouldn't die.

Down vs. synthetic filling. Down is more lightweight than synthetic filling: you can compress it and it will last a long time if properly cared for. However, it is more expensive, useless if you get it wet, and difficult to clean.

Synthetic-filled bags are cheaper and easy to care for, and they still have insulating properties if you get them wet. However, synthetic filling won't last as long as down, and its warmth-to-weight ratio is not as high as down's.

SLEEPING PAD

A sleeping pad protects you from lying on the hard surface of the ground. Besides making your night's sleep much more comfortable, it can also have insulating qualities that are ideal when the ground is cold. Women-specific sleeping pads will have more cushioning and insulation under the hips and feet (cold spots for women). The extra comfort is a personal decision.

I had the women's Therm-a-Rest NeoAir XLite in the regular size, but they also make this in a shorter size that comes down to mid-thigh. If I had to do my hike over again, I would get the shorter size. After hiking all day, I usually put my backpack under my feet at night to elevate them and to reduce any swelling – besides, it just felt good. Other times I would turn on my side and curl my legs up, so I wasn't using the lower part of my sleeping mattress anyway. The shorter mid-thigh size pad would have saved me both pack-weight and the energy to blow it up each night.

What qualities should you consider when choosing a sleeping pad?

Closed-cell foam pad vs. inflatable air mattress. The closed-cell pads are much easier to set up and take down; simply fold yours accordion-style along its creases. However, they fold into a pretty large size – most hikers carry them on the outside of their packs. They are also not as comfortable as an air mattress.

Air mattresses need to be blown up, either by you, a pump or a new funnel system in which you gather air and roll it up into the sleeping pad. They are much more comfortable than the closed-cell foam pads, and you can adjust the amount of air to make them more or less firm. It does take time to blow them up each night and to let the air out every morning.

R-value. R-value measures insulating ability and tells you how well the product will protect you from the cold ground. The higher the R-value, the greater the insulating power of the sleeping pad. Because most women are cold sleepers, women's pads will contain more foam or insulation in the foot and torso areas, generally resulting in a higher R-value.

Weight. The closed-cell foam pads are about the same weight as air mattresses.

Durability. The closed-cell pads are more durable than the air mattresses, as closed cell pads are thick and sturdy while the air mattresses are made of a thinner material, which can be punctured. Most air mattresses come with an emergency repair kit, which should tide you over until you can get to an outfitter to determine if you need further repairs.

SLEEPING BAG LINER

A liner is a thin bag that is used in conjunction with your sleeping bag to add warmth or that can be used by itself in warm weather. I used the Sea to Summit Thermolite Reactor sleeping bag liner which added about 15° of warmth. I kept my liner the entire hike. If it was really cold, I would use it with my sleeping quilt. If it was hot, I would sometimes use it alone without the quilt. I also loved using it as a fitted sheet around my sleeping pad, especially in the summer when it was super hot – this way I would sweat and be stinking on top of the liner and not on my actual pad. I could wash the liner easily – the pad not so much.

PILLOW

Most hikers think they can get by without a pillow and use a heap of bunched up clothing but then end up buying a pillow later. I had the Big Sky International DreamSleeper UltraLight inflatable pillow, which was very light and deflated to the size of a small pocketknife. I am normally a two-pillow sleeper, but still, this pillow worked great for me. I'd often put my buff over it like a pillowcase since buffs can be washed, but the pillow cannot be.

A wide variety of inflatable pillows are on the market. Originally, I wanted to try going without, but at the last minute, my husband and I both bought these pillows, and we were so glad we did. Besides being perfectly comfortable for sleeping, they were great for propping up and reading in our tent at the end of the day.

FOOTWEAR

With oodles of women's trail runners and hiking boots on the market, the most important factor in choosing a good trail shoe or boot is to know your own feet. In general, women's hiking shoes are narrower than men's. Also, women usually have a smaller heel than men, as well as thinner ankles.

To be fitted properly for thru-hiking boots or trail runners, visit an outfitter later in the day. This will give you time to be up and on your feet and to let your feet swell a bit. Most thru-hikers' feet will swell during a thru-hike, so buying a larger than normal size boot or trail runner will help. Wear the exact hiking socks or sock combo that you will wear on your thru-hike. For me, this was Injinji sock liners, followed by Darn Tough lightly padded hiking socks. Tell the outfitter you will be thru-hiking so they know to allow extra room for swelling – a good outfitter will know this. Have them measure both of your feet as they may not be the exact same size.

HIKING BOOTS

Usually made of some kind of leather or Gortex, hiking boots have been around practically forever. A sturdy pair of hiking boots will provide ankle support and traction and will last a long time.

Pros: Boots are durable and provide good ankle support. You won't go through as many pairs of boots as you will trail runners.

Cons: Boots are much heavier and more expensive than trail runners. They require breaking in to avoid blisters and discomfort, which is not convenient when you need your 2nd pair on the trail. Even if they are waterproof, they will eventually take in water on the AT and then will take impossibly long to dry out.

TRAIL RUNNERS

Similar to a tennis shoe, but built sturdier for the rocks, mud, roots and mountains you will encounter on the trail, trail runners are the modern way to thru-hike. I wore the Salomon X-Mission 3's, which I loved – they were light, comfy, and wide enough around my toes, and whenever I got them wet, the mesh uppers allowed them to dry quickly. Since my thru-hike, I have found a brand that works better for me, the Altra Lone Peak 3.0. They have a similar wide toe box but are more comfortable. They are also a zero-drop shoe, so you should research this to decide if this is right for your feet.

Pros: Trail runners are lightweight and quick-drying. You can put them on and take them off quickly. They also breath well so as not to trap moisture, which leads to blisters and other feet problems.

Cons: One pair will only last about 500 miles, maybe more, maybe less (I went through three pairs on my hike) and they don't have any ankle support.

What features should you look for in trail runners?

Waterproofing. Both hiking boots and trail runners come in a waterproof version, but please do NOT get waterproof footwear. I know you're thinking, *But wouldn't I want a waterproof shoe, especially on the AT where I'll be hiking in water and rain so much of the time?*

Actually, because you'll be hiking so often in streams and water and rain and snow, waterproofs are not a good choice for a thru-hike. They may work for the first day or two of water and rain, but eventually, they will become saturated. And then you are up the proverbial creek because the water will not drain out. Your feet will become wet with no ventilation and no chance of drying; this is how you develop trench foot (and also blisters). And when you end your day, your footwear will not even dry overnight because the waterproofing is now working against you. It will take days to dry them out.

Insoles. If you like to have your own insoles in your hiking shoes, go to a reputable shoe or outdoor store to be fitted for them. They can help you choose from the many different kinds, depending on what type of arch your foot has and what your foot needs.

CAMP SHOES

After a day of hiking, change into your camp shoes to let your feet air out and to protect your feet while walking on the forest ground. Typical camp shoes are Crocs (lightweight with air holes) and flip-flops. I had the Xero Z-Trails sandals with straps, which worked great for me. I used them to walk around, both in camp and in town, and to ford the Maine rivers. If I had had foot or blister problems, I could have even hiked in them.

SOCKS

Remember that magical material I told you about earlier? Merino wool is the best material for hiking socks. Non-itch, quick-drying and moisture-wicking are just a few of the great qualities of merino wool. I personally used a two-sock combination. My first layer was the Injinji sock liners, which are thin and literally fit like a glove around each of your toes. The purpose of the material around each of your toes is to prevent your toes from rubbing against each other, which creates blisters. My second layer was the Darn Tough merino wool light-cushioned hiking socks. For me, this two-layer system worked well to prevent blisters. Smartwool is another good brand for merino wool socks among the various brands available.

GAITERS

Gaiters are small pieces of fabric in varied lengths that attach to the outside of your hiking boots or shoes and go up your leg and over your socks. I bought my gaiters from UltraGam on Etsy. She made them out of an eclectic-patterned material which I really loved and got compliments on all the time. Besides being cute, they were functional for keeping dirt, sticks, stones and other debris out of my shoes and for keeping my socks cleaner than they would have been without the gaiters. And best of all, they helped keep ticks from getting on me or in my shoes.

To attach them, there is a hook on the front part of the gaiter that you hook onto your shoelaces. The second place of attachment is a Velcro sticker you place on the back heel of your shoe, which is matched up with a Velcro tab on the gaiter. After a while, the Velcro sticker on the heel of my shoe would come off, so I super-glued it, and this kept it on.

CLOTHING

Clothing is a personal preference, but remember: *layers*. Merino wool in varying thicknesses is good for shirts. You'll want a base layer, a mid-layer and an outer layer.

The base layer is for your hottest days (*i.e.,* T-shirt and shorts).

The mid-layer is placed on top of your base layer for slightly colder hiking days (*i.e.,* long-sleeved, thicker shirt, and leggings or hiking pants).

The outer layer is for super cold hiking days and should be worn over your base and mid-layers (*i.e.,* fleece, puffy or rain jacket and rain pants or skirt). A "puffy jacket" is a hiker term for a warm, synthetic or down-insulated jacket. Get one with a hood. I can't tell you how many times I was happy to have my hood up around me to protect against the wind and cold.

You should also think about what you want to sleep in at night, and don't forget extra layers for sleeping when it is really cold out. I have an Icebreaker T-shirt and my skort, which I also wore for my town clothes, and in the winter had fleece leggings, thick socks and a pullover fleece hoodie. See Chapter 6 for bras and underwear.

You can see my full gear list in the bonus section of this book.

For me, tight-fitting biking shorts were the most comfortable for hiking because they didn't ride up or give me wedgies, and most importantly, they prevented inner-thigh chafing.

Instead of a long-sleeved T-shirt for my mid-layer, I used cycling sleeves (tight fitting sleeves with thumb-holes that stretched from my wrists to my shoulders). I wore my T-shirt as my base layer, and if it got colder, I could easily put my cycling sleeves on while hiking and without taking off my pack. The sleeves, along with the T-shirt, basically made a long-sleeved T-shirt. And when I warmed up, I could just as easily peel them off and stick them in a pocket without stopping. I thought this idea was ingenious! I bought a generic pair from Amazon.com, but I see now that Buffusa.com makes them as well.

RAINWEAR

Rainwear is a tough subject because even though it will keep the rain out, it also will not let your skin "breathe," or more precisely, it stops your sweat from evaporating. Many hikers choose in warm weather to be wet with rain instead of sweat. However, being drenched is miserable and, in some conditions, can cause hypothermia, leaving rainwear the only alternative to keep us reasonably comfortable and safe.

What options do you have for rain protection?

Poncho. A poncho is basically a sturdy garbage sack with a hood – very lightweight, affordable, and sometimes large enough to go over your backpack as well. However, if it's windy out, the poncho can be very uncomfortable to wear. It is usually quite large and not fitted at all, and it will flap around uncontrollably in the wind, which will inevitably let in some rain.

Rain jackets. You can find these in various brands and prices. Get one with pit zips to allow air flow.

Rain pants. These are also available in many different varieties. Some come with zippers on the bottom to easily slide on without taking off your shoes. Frog Toggs makes a very affordable and lightweight jacket and pants.

Rain skirt. Sunsets loved this. It came down almost to his knees, covered his shorts and kept them dry, and allowed sufficient air flow. The rain skirt has several Velcro tabs which make it easy to put on and take off, as well as to close gaps or to leave the bottom open to breathe better. He bought the ULA Equipment brand and it worked great for him. Even when it wasn't raining, we used it as a ground cover during breaks if the only place to sit was on a wet log or the wet ground.

Umbrella. The Euroschirm hiking umbrella (available from Amazon and Zpacks) worked great for me. It isn't a compact umbrella, but I figured out how to put it under my chest strap and hip belt to secure it so I could use it hands-free. Another umbrella available on Amazon attaches to your head; I used this for my 500-mile Camino hike in Spain and it worked great. I also had a rain jacket to use in colder weather, but in the summer, I only used the umbrella, which kept rain off my head and pack without making me hotter than I already was. A rain jacket in the summer can be suffocating and sweltering – you'll likely sweat more than you would get wet with the rain! An umbrella is also good to keep the hot summer sun off you.

Pack cover. Some backpacks come with a rain cover while others do not. You can easily find a pack cover for your size pack (in liters). I used the Sea to Summit cover, which was sufficient.

Pack liner. This is a simple trash compactor bag that you put inside your pack as a liner. It works great to keep water out, especially if you do not have a pack cover, or even if you do, it adds a layer of protection. I suggest choosing a white one instead of black, as it makes it easier to see inside.

COOKWARE

COOK POT

You will need a cook pot for hot drinks, any meals you make with boiling water, and cold meals that you soak in the pot for a while. They are typically made of aluminum or the lighter and pricier option of titanium. A good size for thru-hikers will vary from 700 ml – 900 ml. Options include a lid to cook food faster and plastic-coated handles to avoid burning yourself.

STOVE

A cook stove has one purpose: to boil water, and the faster the better. This is perfect for ramen noodles, rice or pasta sides, instant mashed potatoes and hot chocolate, coffee or tea.

The three most popular stoves are the MSR Pocket Rocket, the Jetboil and the homemade alcohol stove. The first two use a gas canister which is easily found in trail towns. The third stove is homemade from an aluminum can or cat food container and uses liquid fuel, which is also readily found along the trail, but the fuel requires a container and can be messy.

You can also choose not to use a cook stove and to eat only cold food. I did this about halfway through my hike. The stove was sent home, the fuel and lighter were put in a hiker box, and Sunsets and I munched on things like jerky, crackers and cheese, pepperoni or chicken nuggets in tortillas. We loved it. It took so much less work and time at the end of the day. Call us lazy, but we were super tired from hiking all day, and in the middle of summer, the last thing we wanted was to eat hot food.

SPORK

"Spork" is a portmanteau coined from the combination of fork and spoon. All you need is a spoon, and a long-handled titanium one is best because it's lightweight, sturdy, and able to reach into that deep peanut butter jar or instant mashed potato package.

WATER

The contaminants you need to worry about if you do not filter or treat your water include parasites, protozoa, bacteria and viruses. Tainted water can cause diarrhea, vomiting, and stomach cramping, and can sometimes be serious enough to take you off trail completely.

Hikers who choose not to treat their water at all are playing what I call "water roulette." Sure, you can find clean spring water, but certainly not all the time. I'd rather be safe than sorry, and with the lightweight and affordable options these days, why take chances?

What method should you use for treating water on your thru-hike?

Filters. The most common way to treat water is to filter it, which will take care of protozoa and bacteria but will not remove viruses.

The most common filter used and loved by hikers is the Sawyer Squeeze. However, there is a new model Sawyer just came out with – the Micro – which is one ounce lighter and two inches smaller with seemingly the same flow rate.

Tips: if temperatures dip below freezing at night, put your filter in your sleeping bag with you. If it freezes, it will cease to be effective, but you'll have no way of knowing this – that is, until you get sick. Another tip is to keep your filter in a ziplock bag; this will keep any water from dripping on you or your backpack.

Boiling. Yes, boiling your water will kill everything and is very effective at purifying your water. But this is not practical on a thru-hike. Your body will require many liters of water during the day, even more in hot weather. Since water is heavy, you will not want to carry more than two liters at a time (some hikers just carry one liter). You would need to gather and boil water approximately every two to three hours on your hike. Not only will this take time, but it will also take fuel, which is heavy to carry.

Chemicals. Because they are lightweight and take care of all four contaminants, chemicals are a great option. The only con is that the treated water must sit for up to 20 minutes for the chemicals to work. Well, one more con: since you aren't filtering it, the water will sometimes have "floaties" – those particles of dirt, debris and dead things sometimes found in water.

UV light. The SteriPen is the most common form used, and it effectively takes care of all four contaminates by disrupting the DNA and rendering them sterile so they can no longer reproduce. However, the SteriPen only works with clear water, so if the water is cloudy at all, it will first need to be filtered. Next, to hold the water while you stir the UV light, you will need a colored bottle, which is heavier than the typical Smartwater bottles. One more drawback: the light bulb could break or go out, leaving the utensil useless.

SECURING YOUR FOOD

You will need to keep your food safe from bears, rodents and raccoons, but which method should you use for securing your food on your thru-hike?

Bear bag. The most common choice, a bear bag is typically a waterproof bag to hold 8-20 liters, depending on how many days you will hike before resupplying. With a bear-line and a carabiner, you can hang it over a tree branch at a height bears cannot reach; it also needs to be a certain distance from the tree trunk and branch it hangs from since bears can climb. Ironically, the preferred method of hanging on the AT is named for the Pacific Crest Trail, and it worked well for us. Search for "PCT bear bag method" on YouTube for helpful videos on how to hang, and practice this at least once before you start your hike.

Ursack. Made from Kevlar and designed to withstand violent molestation by bears, the Ursack is typically not hung but tied to a tree to keep a bear from easily carrying it away.

Note: I have heard stories – and actually met two people this happened to – of bears actually getting into Ursacks. This is not to deter you from the Ursack, since the same can be said about a poorly hung bear bag. It is just a reminder that gear and systems can fail, and you need to be prepared.

Bear Canister. This is a large, barrel-shaped container with a screw-top lid that secures food. It is not hung, but typically wedged under a fallen tree. Even if the bear can pry the bucket out of its hiding place, the bear will not be able to get inside, and will eventually abandon it.

Bear Roulette. This is the laziest and not-so-smart option. Please don't keep your food in your shelter with you, unless you want a bear to wake you in the middle of the night.

TREKKING POLES

This is a personal preference, but I loved my trekking poles. I had the Leki Corklite Speed Lock trekking poles. To me, they were like having an extra set of limbs that pulled me up mountains, helped me descend steep slopes without falling on my face, provided a gage for how deep the water and mud were on either side of a railroad tie in a bog, and gave me something to lean on heavily when I was tired. Some hikers did not use trekking poles and others used only one instead of two, but the majority of hikers we saw used them and loved them.

GUIDES

The AT Guide by David "Awol" Miller (Awol's *Guide*), the most popular guide used on the trail, is updated each year. You can buy it for northbound or southbound, and as a bound book, loose leaf or a pdf. (TIP: buy the book from his website theatguide.com. It comes with a heavy-duty ziplock bag to protect it. Also, I took this bound book to my local print shop and had it coil bound, which made it easy to keep it open to our current location each day).

The Appalachian Trail Thru-Hiker's Companion by the

Appalachian Long Distance Hikers Association is the official guidebook and is regularly updated.

Guthook's Appalachian Trail is a smartphone app. It is GPS based and broken down into segments, so you don't have the whole app loaded to your phone at once. The app does not use wifi or cell data and works flawlessly in airplane mode. It also will not drain your phone battery. It's basically brilliant. We could always see where we were on the trail (or if we got off the trail, which direction to go to get back to the trail), and most importantly, how many miles were left to camp each night.

Sunsets and I used an effective combination of Awol's *Guide* and the *Guthook's* app, which I heartily recommend. Sometimes I'd take a picture with my phone of the section from the Awol's *Guide* we were going to hike that day, so I could easily glance at it throughout the day instead of hauling out the paper guidebook.

For more information on gear, refer to the Bonus Section of this book where I itemize my full gear list from my thru-hike.

Finally, I give you my *Top 10 Pieces of Gear* – my most loved and appreciated items on my thru-hike!

Chica's Top 10 Pieces of Gear

1. Buff
2. Air pillow
3. Cycling sleeves
4. Cuddl Duds pullover fleece hoodie

5. Gaiters – UltraGam on Etsy

6. RunninGluv (basically a snot and sweat rag)

7. Skort – worn in town and sometimes hiking

8. Water bottle holder – JustinsUL on Etsy

9. Phone holder – Packs

10. Mini Swiss army knife (mainly for the scissors)

11. OTHER TIDBITS & TIPS

Here are a few more helpful tidbits and tips I wanted to include that are not easily categorized.

RUNNINGLUV

A hiker-friend gave me a RunninGluv, a 9" x 9" piece of cloth with one smooth side and the other a bit thicker. Although I (very proudly) became a "snot-rocket" expert on trail (blowing your nose into the woods instead of into a tissue), I still needed to do a little clean up afterwards. The RunninGluv is great for wiping sweat from your face and wiping or blowing your nose. My nose tends to run in the cold and sometimes when I'm working out, so this was the handiest thing for me. I used it all the time – so much better than using my dirty hands. The RunninGluv has a convenient little elastic loop on one end (to place on your thumb so you can twist the fabric around your wrist), which I attached to a small caribiner on the front shoulder strap of my pack. Purchase this fabulous tool on Amazon or on their website (runningluv.com).

BRUSHING TEETH

Before I began my hike, I couldn't fathom how to brush my teeth in the woods with no running water. This tip was given to me by Karma (a different Karma from the one who gave me her backpack), whom you'll meet in Chapter 18.

The answer is … brush your teeth dry! Really, it works. Put a small bit of toothpaste on your brush and start brushing your teeth. It will feel dry and pasty at first, but your saliva will soon add moisture to the process and the toothpaste will bubble and spread around easily. When you finish brushing, spit away from your campsite. If you want, take a swig of water to rinse your mouth, but it isn't necessary. Your teeth will be clean and your mouth will feel extremely fresh.

DRINKING AND TRIPPING

Yep, I had this problem of drinking and tripping. Tripping, that is, while drinking water from my water bottle.

Many hikers use the 1L Smartwater bottle. Made of very sturdy plastic, it will usually hold up for a while; I only replaced it once on my whole hike. This size bottle comes with a screw cap.

For this klutzy girl, the screw-cap did not work well at all. I had to hold the bottle with one hand and take the cap off with the other, which was hard to do when both hands had a trekking pole in them. Then, I would take a sip, but as I did this, I needed to raise my head, which subsequently took my eyes off the ground. I'd inevitably trip unless I stopped hiking and stood completely still. If I didn't drop a trekking pole to begin with, I'd usually slosh water all over myself and trip and fall. It was a disaster!

What worked well for me was to replace the screw cap with a "squirt-top cap" (a bottle cap with a tip you can pull up to squirt the water into your mouth). You can find this squirt-top cap on the 750 ml Smartwater bottle, but it will also fit the 1L size.

With the squirt-top cap, I didn't have to stop. I didn't pour water all over myself. And most importantly, I never tripped. This may not sound like a big deal, but you drink so much water on the trail, you'll want to hike and drink on the go without having to stop every time you take a sip. You might be much more coordinated than I am; if so, you can just hike right by this tip.

Another helpful tip involving the water squirt-top cap is it can be used for back flushing the Sawyer Squeeze Water Filter. Anytime you can use a piece of gear for multiple purposes is a win/win. The Sawyer Squeeze comes with a syringe for back flushing it (a process you will need to do from time to time to clean out the filter). However, leave the syringe at home, and you can use the little squirt-top instead. To the see the specifics of how to do this, search YouTube for "Sawyer Squeeze backflush with Smartwater cap."

SHOE GOO

Shoe Goo, a thick, magical glue specifically for shoes, works better than super glue. I used it many times on my trail runners to fill in holes or gaps that suddenly materialized. You can frequently find Shoe Goo in the hiker boxes. Just use what you need and put the tube back in the box for the next hiker.

HITCH HIKING

You may think hitch hiking was a thing of the past, but it is common along the Appalachian Trail and thru-hiker community. It is legal in 13 of the 14 states along the trail (the outcast is New York). You will often need to hitch hike to get from the trail into towns. You don't want to hike an extra two to five miles on concrete if you don't have to!

This is where women win! Most guys like to have a woman hitch with them. Why? Because guys tend to look rough and unkempt – those long, straggly, untrimmed beards are the culprit. But if they are with a woman, even though we stink just as much, we usually have a better appearance, so people are more willing to pick us up for a ride. Women give the men credibility.

EXTREME TEMPERATURES

Overheating. While the sun and heat can affect everyone differently, Sunsets is extremely sensitive to heat. A few things that help: dip your buff or T-shirt in a stream and wring it out and put it back on; go for a swim; drink more water; stop and take frequent breaks in the shade. We stopped once every hour in the heat of the summer. Also, wear a sunhat and sunscreen. Some people wear a long-sleeved shirt and long pants for sun protection; some brands have sunscreen built into them.

Also, we both used a "cool rag," a small towel that you dip in cold or warm water, wring out briefly, and then whip in the air to cool it down. Then you can put it over your head, around your neck, or wherever you are most heated, and keep hiking. As long as the rag is wet, you can whip it to cool it again.

In the heat, you will sweat and lose salt at a high rate, so to protect yourself against dehydration and muscle cramps, add electrolyte mixes to your water, eat salty snacks, and for potassium, consume bananas and coconut water.

Hypothermia. A condition in which your body loses heat faster than it can produce it, hypothermia is a dangerous threat to any hiker in windy or wet, cool conditions. As soon as you experience any symptoms of hypothermia (shivering, mumbling, weak pulse, shallow breathing, clumsiness, low energy, confusion), stop at a shelter or put up your tent, strip and change into dry clothes, put on all your warm layers, and get inside your sleeping bag. If you have an emergency blanket, put it on. Drinking anything hot will help warm your body from the inside out.

POOPER SCOOPER

Doing the do in the woods is a necessity during a thru-hike, so you'll need to dig a cathole. Instead of the typical $20 trowel, a 9" aluminum snow tent stake is about the same weight and much more affordable, and it works great! We also kept extra paracord wound around the handle, which added leverage for digging and also was handy if we needed paracord for anything. Some say having a digging tool is unnecessary, but digging a 6" cathole with a stick or trekking pole is no easy feat.

RESUPPLYING

Can I resupply along the trail exclusively, or do I need to have packages sent to myself? One of the advantages of thru-hiking the Appalachian Trail as opposed to other long hikes (like the PCT) is that you can obtain supplies all along the AT without having to send packages to yourself. Two great resources for locating resupply places are Awol's

Guide and *Appalachian Trail Clarity*:

https://appalachiantrailclarity.com/2016/03/15/appalachian-trail-thru-hiker-resupply-points/

How do I figure out how many days of food I need to carry? First, you will need to know how many days until you want to stop again for more food and how many miles you average each day. Then, using Awol's *Guide,* estimate where you will be and locate a resupply place close to that spot. Count how many meals and snacks you need until you reach the next resupply location.

For example, I am currently in Hot Springs, NC and I want to resupply in five days. I'm currently averaging 12-13 miles a day, so in five days (5 x 13 = 65) I will be 65 miles further on the trail. According to Awol's *Guide*, that puts me a few miles past Erwin, TN where there are ample supplies AND a hostel for a shower and laundry (yea!). Okay, I'll stop in Erwin, but until then, I will need five granola bars for breakfast, 10 full size Snickers for snacks (hey, don't judge me – I eat two a day on trail, it's a good source of protein), 5 tortillas with pepperoni and cheese for lunch (will share a package of tortillas with my husband), *etc*. That's how I know how much food to buy in Hot Springs. I'll repeat this process in Erwin where I will also indulge in buying too much candy and hopefully grab a glass of wine somewhere.

SLACK-PACKING

Simply put, slack-packing is hiking with only those things you need for the day. Without the load of your full pack weight, you can conceivably hike more miles at a faster rate.

You will only carry a few essentials (water filter, snacks, first aid, rain coat, *etc.*). You can either retrieve your full pack at a road crossing or parking lot later in the day (to camp out in the woods) or be driven to a hostel for the night. The point is you have help, so you only need to carry a tiny pack instead of your full-weight one. Hostels that offer slack-packing will typically have loaner daypacks for you to use.

Slack-packing is surprisingly easy to coordinate – you can do this typically with hostel owners who are well aware of the trail and different drop-off and pick-up points. They will arrange a pick up time (or ask you to call) at the end of the day. This can also be done with friends and family, of course. You just need to find a good trailhead for drop-off and pick-up locations, and you're good to go.

I loved slack-packing! We took advantage of it when weather or illness would have otherwise sidelined us. With super-light packs on our backs, we felt like we were flying.

POST-TRAIL DEPRESSION

Unfortunately, post-trail depression is a real thing. People love the trail life so much that they find it hard to go back to ordinary life. The best advice I can give you is that knowledge and awareness of this ahead of time is half the battle. Being prepared to experience any kind of depression after your long-distance hike is better than being hit with it out of the blue. Another instance of the positive power of negative thinking.

While you are still on the trail, try these tips to help prevent post-trail depression:

• Start planning another hike (of any kind) so you have something new and fun to anticipate. There's many different trails in the US alone to consider a thru-hike of (PCT, CDT, Arizona Trail, Colorado Trail, *etc.*).

• Ask yourself how you might stay connected to the trail, and imagine how you might follow through after your hike. For instance, maybe you would like to try hiking it again but in a different way, or you might help maintain the trail or do other related volunteer work. Helping other hikers with trail magic could be your calling, or you may decide to share your experience through writing, blogging, podcasts, or videos.

• Being excited about a new venture or other change in your future will help immensely. This is very personal, so only you know what it might be. It could be anything – starting a new garden in your backyard, moving to a new house or city, writing a book, starting a new job, volunteering at an animal shelter – it just needs to be something new and exciting for *you*. You may be on this thru-hike because of a major change that is already taking place in your life. If the change is something you dread, your time on the AT may provide an opportunity to plan for a better outcome.

• While you are hiking the AT, make sure you are connected with your tramily via social media or email. After your hike is done, staying in touch with friends who understand the trail and all you've been through will help.

IV: CONVERSATIONS WITH BADASS WOMEN HIKERS

"She believed she could, so she did."

– R.S. GREY

Any woman who steps foot on the Appalachian Trail and does any length of a hike is amazing. But a woman who hikes the whole damn 2,200-mile Appalachian Trail? TOTAL. COMPLETE. 100%. BADASS.

The remarkable women I interviewed for my book all recently hiked all or most of the Appalachian Trail. I admire each of them immensely. Each has her own story to tell with a different set of circumstances. I hope you enjoy them as much as I do.

JEN BECK SEYMOUR

12. CRAYOLA (Celia)

I first met Crayola early on in our hike. She was a solo hiker, but at the time was hiking with a three-person tramily. I remembered her because she was the nicest person of that tramily – and also because of her green hair!

Then many months lapsed when we didn't see her at all. Finally, in the last state, Maine, we saw her on the top of a mountain where she was taking a break, and we had a reunion. It's very odd to meet someone briefly, not see them for months, and then run into them later, and it's like seeing a long-lost friend – the bonds seem tighter when out in the wilderness. She summited Katahdin just a couple days before us and got a badass tattoo of her trail name afterwards.

Instagram: @adventuresofcrayola

Tell me a bit about yourself.

I'm 30 years old. I grew up in NC, not far from the AT, but I have been living in Portland, Oregon for 11 years. I hiked the AT from March 25, 2017 to September 14, 2017, northbound.

How did you decide to hike the AT?

Hiking the AT had always been a dream of mine. My father completed about 2,000 miles of it in two long section hikes in the mid-1970s. When I was a child, he would take me up to Carver's Gap near Roan Mountain and point out the white blazes and talk about how it feels to walk all the way to Maine.

I decided to finally do it after the breakup of a long-term relationship. I had talked to my partner about my desire to hike the trail, and his response was always, "But what will *I* do?" My life revolved around his needs. So when he dumped me without warning on my 28th birthday, my first thought, after the initial blow, was that at least I could finally do that hike that I had wanted to do for so long.

Did you hike the AT alone? Did you leave family, and how did you cope with missing them? Did you have a tramily at any point?

I did hike the AT alone. I don't have family in Portland, but I do have a really tight-knit group of amazing friends and a wonderful dog. Some of my friends were going through some stressful times when I left and I felt guilty for leaving them. But they were supportive. They even wrote me tons of letters while I was out there.

I had a tramily for about the first 700 miles. I did enjoy having a tramily and I was sad when it broke apart. However, by that point I had the confidence and drive to keep going on my own. I almost always knew someone at whatever shelter I stayed at, and sometimes I would even plan to meet up with people in the evening, but the majority of the actual hiking was done alone. Once I was more confident on the AT, I honestly liked hiking more without a tramily. With a tramily or hiking partner, there may be days that they don't feel like doing as many miles as you do, or vice versa. You may want a rest day when they don't, or they may need to go into town for resupply when you don't. I feel like once I was on my own, I was able to cover more miles because I could go further when I felt good or stop short when I needed rest.

You will often find that you keep running into the same people even if you don't follow each other's every move. I ended up finishing the trail with a group of people who I had consistently seen almost every day since Pennsylvania. We weren't a strict trail family, but we did occasionally share meals and accommodations in town and sometimes hiked together on the trail.

Did you have any hiking or overnight camping experience before hiking the AT?

As I mentioned, backpacking in general (and the AT specifically) was dearly loved by father, so he often took my brother and I on section hikes as children. But I had never been on my own before starting the AT, and the last time I had been backpacking at all was when I was a teenager.

Did you ever feel unsafe or threatened by a person, animal, or situation?

There were times that I felt scared about injuries, falls or animals. Honestly, I'm really scared of cows, and I was so relieved when I saw the Guthook's marker "last pasture for northbounders." There was also a time that two bears were chasing each other through the woods and not paying attention and almost ran into me. I camped illegally at a SNP (Shenandoah National Park) way post that night to avoid being in the backcountry.

I think the most unsafe I felt though was around men, and especially non-hiker men. There were a few times that I encountered men at road crossings who were definite creeps, but there were also times that I think men made well-meaning comments that they didn't intend to be creepy. Men at road crossings might ask things like, "Where are your friends? Were those people in front of you your family? How far are you going today? Any good camp spots up ahead?" I think it was typically out of genuine interest in hiking or puzzlement at seeing a woman alone in the back country, but I wish men understood that the way it feels to me is that they are asking if I am alone and where they can find me later. In the event that I had to camp alone, I absolutely avoided camp spots near roads and sometimes slept with my knife in my hand.

Did the AT change you? If so, how?

It definitely changed me for the better. Before the trail, I didn't care if I died. I wasn't suicidal, but I just didn't care about life. I was totally apathetic. I was taking care of other people's needs, both at work and in my personal life. In short, I had lost my power. I wasn't able to take control of my life and get what I wanted out of it. Hiking the AT empowered me. I learned that I can accomplish things that are important to me. I can get my body healthy. I can change the things that are not making me happy. I also learned to be present in the moment and appreciate every day.

Please explain the origin of your trail name.

I got my trail name because my hair was green. I also had brightly colored rain gear and base layers. And I have, um, colorful language. I was scared that I would get the trail name "Green" because of my hair, and then everyone would assume I smoked a lot of weed (I don't, at all), but also I learned that you don't have to accept a trail name just because someone suggests it.

After the AT, I got a crayon tattoo on my arm. So on the PCT (Pacific Crest Trail, which I hiked a good portion of in 2018), one of the first questions most people asked is "What came first, the tattoo or the name?"

What was the most unexpected thing that happened or that you experienced?

Honestly, the most unexpected thing for me was probably all the relationships I formed. I hadn't done much up-to-date research on hiking the AT and hadn't followed blogs or vlogs at all. I went out with the perception that I would be alone most of the time or be around people that I didn't relate to. A part of me probably hoped that I would be alone since I was at possibly the lowest point in my life beforehand, and I felt like I deserved loneliness so I might as well get used to it. I ended up making dozens of wonderful friends, many of whom I am still in frequent contact with a year later.

Favorite hiker trash or funny moment?

I love being hiker trash. I like to think I've always been trash and I finally found the specific type of trash I'd like to be. I love packing way too many people into a tent or shelter or hotel room. I love hitchhiking. I even love that hiker trash stink. I loved taking a freezing cold shower in the dark outdoor shower at the Graymoor Friary with my headlamp on and a Peach-a-rita in hand. I loved overhearing the tourists on Mt. Washington say things like, "How did all the homeless people afford the train up here?" and "Why are there so many people with backpacks? Can you *walk* up here?!"

What was your favorite trail food?

I was lucky, in that my hugely supportive parents made home-dehydrated meals for me, which gave me a lot more variety in my meal planning. One of my favorites was mexican rice with dehydrated beans, which I would add to tortillas with cheese and hot sauce to make burritos. I also became totally obsessed with Sweetart Chewy Sours and would buy them by the pound whenever they were available.

Did you have any injuries?

Nothing serious. I had a lot of knee pain at the start until I dropped my pack weight and lost a considerable amount of body weight, and later on I had some falls that left me bruised and bloody. I also struggled to keep my weight up towards the end of my hike.

This year (2018), I attempted a thru-hike of the PCT and had to take so much time off due to injuries and illness that I was only able to complete about 1400 miles of the trail. Your feet may change on a hike, so don't be afraid to switch shoes if yours are no longer working for you. And make sure to boil water for three times as long if you're at high elevation and your water filter fails (which won't be an issue on the AT but could be on other trails that go to higher elevation).

How did you feel on the day you finished your hike?

People ask this question a lot and honestly, even a full year later, it's still really hard for me to concisely verbalize how I felt that day. I felt strange, I guess. I had thought a lot about what it would be like to make it to that sign on Katahdin. During the last few weeks, just thinking about it made me tear up. I thought I would cry. Or feel completed. Or both. But honestly, I don't know how to describe what I felt. When I arrived there, it felt unreal. I didn't even want to touch the sign at first. But I did feel done, and I was ready to go home.

How was hiking the AT empowering for you as a woman?

A lot of people, both on and off trail, will discourage you. When I started, I was overweight and carrying far too much gear. Other hikers would make disparaging comments about how slow I was or express disbelief that I could make it to Maine. And in general society, as well as on trail, patriarchy wants to control our bodies. There can be a perception that women shouldn't be athletes at all, or at least shouldn't be outdoors, on their own, in the wilderness. People will judge your body and try to limit you.

Hiking the AT empowered me to take control of my own body and my life and taught me that I can do whatever I set my mind to. As someone who, like many women, has often struggled with body image, I also found it empowering to focus on what my body can do rather than how it may look. Too fat or too skinny becomes irrelevant when your body can climb mountains, day after day. It felt freeing to stop worrying about armpit hair and chubby thighs and just focus on climbing mountains.

It was also inspiring to be around so many amazing hiker-women. The women that I met on trail were so strong and so determined, and some days just being around them gave me strength.

What was hardest thing about your hike?

I think the hardest thing about long-distance hiking is learning to be alone with yourself and your thoughts. Without the distractions of constant access to TV, social media, *etc.,* I spent an excessive amount of time in my own head. I truly believe that many people quit because they can't stand being around themselves that much, and I think that's sad. Sometimes I was so sick of my thoughts circling around in my head, but I also feel like I was able to work through a lot of things and come out of the hike as a better person.

Were there any sacrifices you had to make prior to pursuing your thru-hike?

I can't recall any sacrifices that I made prior to the thru-hike. I suppose I worked 60-80 hours a week to help me save money, but as a newly recovering workaholic, it's likely that I would have been working that much anyway. I was just spending my money on gear instead of stuff I didn't need.

There have been unplanned sacrifices caused by hiking. Prior to my AT hike, I had a close group of friends, seven of us total. While I was on the AT, two of those friends basically fell off. I didn't hear from them at all the whole time, and when I got home, I learned that they had a falling out with some others in the group and had split off. We never repaired our friendship. The same thing happened with one of the remaining friends this summer while I was on the PCT. I worry about my friendships in Portland being impacted by my long stretches of time away from home. Also, while many of my friends are interested in day hikes or car camping trips with me, I find that I often don't have time for friends of mine who have no interest in being outside. And travelling so often has likely made it difficult to form and maintain an intimate partnered relationship.

Did you have any fears or concerns before your hike? If so, how did you deal with them on trail, and how do you feel about them now?

My biggest fear was probably that I would fail, or specifically that I would fail by giving up. I was worried that I would get to the trailhead at the approach trail, panic, and just ask my dad to drive me back home with my tail between my legs. I even turned around to look back halfway up that staircase at Amicalola, but he had already driven off, so I kept going. I was definitely lacking in confidence for probably the first two months. It was most intense the first few weeks, when I would lie awake at night, thinking anxious thoughts like "What am I doing out here?!" and "Is this the right thing for me?" These feelings were intensified by the fact that I was very slow at the beginning.

Eventually, I made the decision to stop thinking about Katahdin, and just focus on the next day or even the next hour. I decided that regardless of whether or not I finished my hike, I would spend six months on the AT and try to enjoy every bit of it. Once I was able to relax, the anxiety melted away and I started to just have a really good time.

I also had a fear about sleep walking. At home, I occasionally sleep walk, and I was afraid that if I were to sleep walk on the trail, I might not find my way back. I ended up being way too tired most days to have the typical sleep issues that I have when I'm in town. I don't know if it was the physical activity, the lack of city noises or the fact that for the first time I was on a regular sleep schedule (rather than a shift work sleep schedule), but I didn't have any of my usual issues with sleep.

Did you have any post-trail depression? If so, how did you get through it?

I definitely had post-trail depression. I think part of that is just that your body gets accustomed to 8-12 hours of exercise a day, and you get addicted to the endorphins that are being released. I can't figure any way that I could possibly get that much exercise in my normal life, where I work 8- to 16-hour shifts in a cubicle type setting. I wish I could tell you that I came up with some fabulous solution for PTD, but I didn't. I felt so dead and apathetic every day when I pulled into the parking garage near my work and pulled my parking pay stub out of the automated machine, that I decided to fully quit my job and hike the PCT this year. Some things that helped or would have helped though, short of planning another thru-hike, include getting outside for day hikes, trying to stay active, keeping in touch with trail friends, and giving back to the hiker community. This year, I plan to get more involved with trail maintenance crews (on the PCT, since it's close to home).

Do you view life differently in any way after hiking the trail?

I definitely do. Before the trail, I felt trapped and powerless. On the trail, I learned that most problems have a solution. If you can't change the actual issue, you can at least change how you feel about it. I feel empowered now to make decisions for myself without putting others first. As an example, when I returned from the trail, I had a new manager at my job. We did not get along, and I was miserable. Other managers knew she was a terrible boss and for months kept telling me, "Just wait, things will get better." But I didn't want to wait for external factors to change so I could be happy. Whereas previously, I would have likely suffered through it or switched jobs, this time I decided to quit my job entirely and hike again. It was my first time being totally unemployed since before I was 16 years old, and I don't think I would have been confident enough to make a decision like that before the trail. Basically I feel like hiking the AT left me with the belief that everything will work out if you just let it. The world can be a beautiful place; you just have to look for the beauty sometimes.

If you could give your newbie hiker self any advice before starting the trail, what would it be?

Don't focus on getting to Maine (or Georgia). To walk 2,200 miles is a massive endeavor, and the miles will come slowly at first. If you focus on an end goal that is months away, it can feel like a daunting task. Instead, focus on daily successes and small gifts that the trail provides each day. Getting a little stronger and more sure-footed every day, finding a leaf that is the perfect shade of gold, eating the best town food, meeting a new friend, taking an unplanned break at a beautiful view: these are the little things that can keep you going when it's raining and your feet hurt.

I also think it's important to be kind to yourself. Take unplanned breaks. Treat yourself (within your budget) in towns. If you're having a bad day, take a break. One day in Rangeley, Maine, with just 200 miles left to go, I stopped by a hostel to pick up some new shoes I had ordered and I found out that they had not arrived. My shoes were so worn out and my feet had been aching, so I was looking forward to those new shoes for weeks. In that moment, even with only 200 miles to go, I almost felt like quitting. The hostel owner offered me a ride into Rangely, and even though I had no reason to go there, I accepted. I got a massive plate of nachos and an imperial pint of beer and after that afternoon off, I was ready to get back on trail and finish strong.

What are your top tips or advice for women wanting to thru-hike the AT?

You should absolutely do it! Have fun and don't take it too seriously. If something isn't working for you, switch it up! Trail-fam dynamic took a turn? Join a different group or hike alone for a bit! Constant rain getting you down? Take an unplanned town day to dry your socks out! Long days stressing you out? Start taking more breaks at beautiful spots! People often create their own problems by being inflexible. For every issue, there is typically a simple way to solve it; you just have to be open to it.

Anything else you'd like to mention?

At risk of being too cliché, hike your own hike. People will tell you how you need to hike. There is no specific formula for a perfect thru-hike. There is a tendency for more experienced (or even less experienced) hikers to insist on certain things: "You have to stay at this hostel. You should wear these shoes. You have to have this baseweight. You must eat at this buffet." It's all bullshit. Do what makes you happy and find what works for you.

13. SWISSMISS (Manuela "Wella" Jay)

I remember hearing from a friend about SwissMiss and her husband, Hook, before we actually met them. Then shortly afterwards, we ran into them on the trail. We spent a cold night with them and another hiker, Jaws, on the top of a mountain above tree line – a memorable experience because I was a stickler about hanging our bear bags every night, and this particular night, we could find absolutely no tall trees in which to hang them. I was freaking out about it, and I asked SwissMiss how they were going to hang their bear bags, and she just laughed and thought I was joking. I relaxed more after that, knowing that at least there were other people with us if we did encounter a bear. I think that was the first (and only) night we kept our bags in our tent vestibule and, surprisingly, slept pretty well.

SwissMiss also spent some time hiking solo in 2018 on the Colorado Trail, conquering any small fears she had of hiking by herself.

YouTube: YouTube.com/c/jaysonthetrail
Instagram: Instagram.com/jaysonthetrail

Tell me a bit about yourself.

My name is Manuela "Wella" Jay (trail name: SwissMiss). I was born and raised in Switzerland (hence my trail name) and moved to the United States a little over 10 years ago. My husband, Justin, (trail name: Hook) and I have lived in Alaska since 2012 with no plans to leave anytime soon (we love the land of the midnight sun and having abundant wilderness at our backdoor).

Justin and I hiked the AT in 2017 via an organization called Warrior Expeditions (www.warriorexpeditions.org). The non-profit organization was founded in 2012 by Marine veteran Sean Gobin. After returning from one of his numerous combat tours, Sean decided to hike the AT to "hike off the war." Sean experienced great relief from his combat-related trauma through long-distance hiking, which is what inspired him to start his non-profit organization and to offer the alternative healing approach of long-distance hiking to fellow veterans. Justin and I are both Army veterans having deployed to Afghanistan in 2013 (Manuela) and 2016 (Justin), although most people on the trail thought I was supporting my military husband as *he* hiked off the war. I learned that there still seems to be a great misconception about women in service and it is widely unknown that we do, in fact, serve on the front lines.

Justin and I felt very fortunate to have been two of the 10 people selected to hike the trail from a pool of 300-plus applicants. We were the first married couple to thru-hike the trail through Warrior Expeditions, which was a great motivator for us to do well and finish the trail, so we wouldn't ruin the chances for future couples to hike together. We started the trail on March 17th, 2017 at Amicalola Falls in Georgia and summited Mt. Katahdin in Maine on September 14th, 2017, making us NOBO thru-hikers.

How did you decide to hike the AT?

Frankly, I had not heard about the Appalachian Trail until I met Justin in 2012. He spent his childhood growing up along the East Coast and had spent much of his teenage years section-hiking the trail. Having grown up in Switzerland, I spent much of my childhood in the woods and the Alps. Hiking and spending time in the outdoors was a big part of my upbringing, for which I am so grateful. Justin had always dreamed of thru-hiking the AT but it was logistically impossible while we were both on active duty. We both separated from the Army in 2016 after reaching our contract commitments and the former dream of thru-hiking suddenly became an actual possibility. By 2016 I was a lot more familiar with the AT, and quite interested in thru-hiking it myself. We saw this transitional time in our lives as the perfect time to recover from deployment and also as a way for us to transition from the military to the civilian world. At the beginning of our hike, we were unsure of what our life in the civilian world would look like, but by the time we reached the summit of Mt. Katahdin, we were stronger as a couple – more relaxed, recovered – and we had a pretty good idea of what we wanted our next chapter in life to look like.

Tell me some positives and negatives regarding hiking with your spouse.

We spent an extensive amount of time watching YouTube videos and reading about other couples as well as talking to couples that had successfully thru-hiked the AT. We tried to listen to their advice and to avoid some of the mistakes they made.

Although we decided to go on this journey together, it was always important to us that we could still hike our own hike. We wanted to have a chance to process our individual baggage and face our demons alone. The approach that worked best for us (and it is truly different for every couple) was to start and end at the same point every day but to hike mostly alone throughout the day. Justin is a faster hiker than I am so he would generally hike ahead of me and we would link up every 30mins – 1 hr. This allowed us to share experiences but still have alone time, which was very important to our overall happiness.

As for the things that kept us happy and sane on the trail:

1. We always carried our own food. After a few days on trail, your entire life starts to revolve around your next snack or town-meal, and we did not want to share a food bag and then get into a fight over who ate the last Snickers bar. Carrying our own individual food bags was essential. In addition to that, Justin quickly learned that I generally packed too little food, so Justin would always have secret, extra "Wella rations" in his bag to keep the hangries at bay (I get very moody or angry when I am hungry). He saved me from having a meltdown on multiple occasions by presenting me with a chocolate bar that seemingly appeared out of nowhere at just the perfect moment. He was definitely my food-angel.

2. We made sure to give each other space by not constantly hiking together.

3. We practiced (and continue to practice) a very candid and open communication style with one another. While this can be difficult at times, it really helped us stay honest and address issues as they came up rather than holding on to resentments which could have compromised our entire hike.

Positives:

• Hiking with Justin was an amazing experience. While we both had good and bad days, it seemed like one hiker was having a good day when the other was not and this allowed us to better support one another and to be there for the other person when they needed it most. I think hiking together played a big part in our ability to finish the trail.

• I love that we shared this life-changing experience together. Now when we talk about the trail, I know exactly what Justin is referencing and we can both reminisce together. It also made our post-trail transition a lot smoother and really helped us ward off post-trail depression because we are constantly surrounded by another AT hiker.

• Hiking together for six months and being exposed to a wide array of weather, stink, dirt, emotions, environments, *etc.*, tested our individual limits and made us stronger as a couple. If you can hike together for that amount of time and still love one another at the end of it, you can do anything together! It showed us how strong we are together and what amazing things we can achieve if we combine our efforts.

Negatives:

While this might sound cliché, I really cannot think of a negative of hiking as a couple. Had we not done as much research as we did or laid some ground-rules prior to hiking, I imagine our experience might have been a lot different, but we had a wonderful experience. Justin is my best friend and adventure-partner and I cannot wait to tackle the next adventure or trail with him.

Did you have a tramily at any point?

As part of hiking through Warrior Expeditions, we spent the first one to two weeks hiking with the other eight hikers that were sponsored through the same program. After reaching Franklin, NC, our group dispersed and Justin and I spent a lot of our time hiking alone, which we quite enjoyed. As we got into the Shenandoahs, we started to hike with one of our fellow Warrior Expeditions friends, Jaws, and ended up spending the rest of our hike with him. I guess you could say we became a mini-tramily although we still spent our days hiking alone at large.

Did you have any hiking or overnight camping experience before hiking the AT?

Yes. Prior to hiking, Justin and I spent quite a bit of time in the Alaska backwoods on overnight camping or hiking trips. We also thru-hiked the Foothills Trail as our "shakedown" hike in order to get used to sleeping in the outdoors together over a prolonged period of time. Spending time in the woods on overnight trips definitely helped to prepare me mentally and to take the edge off of the fear I had of sleeping in the outdoors.

Did you ever feel unsafe or threatened by a person, animal, or situation?

Ninety-nine percent of the time we felt completely safe on trail. There was one incident where we were hiking in Virginia and stopped at a shelter for lunch – there was a man sitting there that clearly did not look like a hiker. He had on brand new clothes (regular street clothes, not hiking gear). He carried an empty backpack with him and a sleeping mat. He was acting very nervous, would only answer our questions in one-word phrases and was shaky. He gave us goosebumps, and the not good kind. Although he never threatened us, we ended up leaving that shelter immediately and reported him to the police shortly after.

The trail is extremely safe, but it is always good to trust your gut feeling and report things when they seem out of sorts. When we reported him to the police, we were notified that multiple people had called about him as well, and he was thought to be a suspect on the loose. Just follow your gut feeling; make sure people know where you are and you will be fine.

Did the AT change you? If so, how?

It showed me that people are inherently good. We received an overwhelming amount of support during our hike, mostly from complete strangers. It re-shaped how I see the world and people at large, and I now believe that, more often than not, people are inherently good.

After carrying everything we needed on our backs for six months, it helped us reconsider what was important in life.

When Justin and I returned to Alaska, we moved into a smaller apartment than we had previously lived in and downsized our belongings by at least one-third. We became more aware of our impact on the world and started to recycle and decided to have only one car. We have been making an effort to spread the word about the benefits of nature therapy via speaking engagements at REI, NPR, *etc.* We switched to a plant-based diet (Justin still eats meat, but only if he hunts it) to lower our impact on the environment, to reduce factory farming and to improve our overall health. Nowadays we put an emphasis on "being here, now." We spend money on experiences, not things. We spend every moment we can outside. We make more time for friends and family.

The AT enhanced our quality of life dramatically and also opened our eyes to a whole new world of adventure, trails and opportunities that are out there.

Please explain the origin of your trail name.

I was born and raised in Switzerland, which is why I got my name, SwissMiss. I should mention that I got MANY other trail names prior to that one that were a lot less flattering: Mary Poppins (which was later changed to Mary Poopins by some jokester because they thought it was funny that I used the restroom so frequently), Dr. Quinn (I helped pop a lot of blisters), *etc.* I liked SwissMiss the most and accepted it as my trail name. Thank goodness we are allowed to deny trail names if we don't like them – I cannot imagine being stuck with Mary Poopins for the entire trail!

Did you have any injuries?

No. I feel very fortunate that I did not get injured throughout my hike. I think proper footwear, using hiking poles and taking it slow (we hiked 12-15 miles on average per day) really helped keep my body unharmed.

You and your husband made videos throughout your hike. Was that hard to do and to keep up with?

We started recording our hike in order to share our journey with our families in the USA and Switzerland. Having a purpose to film kept us motivated to continue filming throughout our hike. I should add that Justin is our tech guru. Had it not been for him, I would not have filmed any of the hike. I felt overwhelmed by technology and was not very comfortable in front of the camera at first. I am so glad he took charge of that part of our hike. As we got further into our hike, the act of recording really helped us, because it gave our day some structure and also gave us a purpose, especially as our YouTube following grew. We felt a responsibility to keep people updated. Looking back, we are so glad we filmed our hike. It is a wonderful way to relive the trail and to share the journey with people that may never be able to set foot on trail.

What was the most unexpected thing that happened or that you experienced?

Justin and I were absolutely blown away by the random acts of kindness we received throughout our hike. I think the military and today's news and social media shape the world in a way that makes it seem dark and portrays people to be selfish and cruel. The incredible kindness we experienced from complete strangers during our hike, however, really changed the way we see the world and people at large. Today we believe that most people are inherently good. We received random acts of kindness in many forms that ranged from having a stranger give us a water bottle or carry out our trash to having complete strangers open up their homes to us after just having met them. The kindness and support we received was positively overwhelming, and we see the world in a new light.

Favorite hiker trash or funny moment?

Near the Tennessee-Virginia border, Justin got food poisoning from a pack of corn tortillas we purchased at the dollar store in Hampton, TN (50 tortillas for $1 is NEVER a good idea – that should have been a warning to us). At 3:00 a.m. the following morning, Justin jumped out of his sleeping bag as the corn tortillas made their presence known. After walking several miles to the nearest road, we made it into town and spent two days holed up in a hostel. Once he sufficiently recovered, we returned to the trailhead and hiked the 21-plus miles into Damascus, our longest day yet. Because Justin had hardly been able to eat for three days and wasn't in the mood for granola bars or ramen, we decided to celebrate entering Virginia by treating ourselves to Mexican food.

Later that evening, I began feeling that something was not right and immediately suspected food poisoning from the Mexican food. Interestingly enough, Justin ate the exact same dish I ate and did not feel sick. Our theory is that the only reason he did not get sick is because he took a swig of moonshine that the storeowner at the local outfitter offered him. Moral of the story – 50 tortillas for $1 from the Dollar General is probably too good to be true. Also, don't pass up free moonshine.

Favorite trail food?

Chili Ramen. It never. Gets. Old!

How did you feel on the day you finished your hike?

We felt incredibly happy and amazed that we had actually made it. There were many people that doubted our ability to hike as a couple and make it all the way. We had many naysayers tell us we would get a divorce by the end of our hike. Finishing felt like both a statement to ourselves and the world – it was incredible. Although we enjoyed our six months of hiking, we were also glad to be done and to move on to new adventures and challenges and, most importantly, running water and the convenience of flushing toilets.

How was hiking the AT empowering for you as a woman?

The trail does not discriminate against age, gender or race. On the trail we are all the same and the playing field is even for all of us. In a world where women are constantly told that we are not enough of something, hiking the AT was a statement and reminder to myself that I AM powerful, I AM strong, I AM beautiful.

In the noise of today's social media and news, it is easy to forget that. I have never felt more beautiful than I do when I am out in nature. I loved that it was ok to be smelly, that no one cared if I hadn't showered in a week or whether or not my nails were about to fall off. As a matter of fact, all of those things were viewed as "badass" on trail by men and women alike. Some girls shaved their heads; some women chose to grow out their leg hair; men wore girls' leggings –

there were no rules. While I enjoyed my own hiking experience, I was also incredibly inspired by the women around me. They were all so strong and beautiful – it was like walking with a tribe of Amazons. All of us looked different. All of us smelled awful. All of us had legs the size of tree trunks from all the muscle we gained. I loved seeing myself and the women around me grow stronger and more confident. I loved learning that I wouldn't die if I slept in the woods. I loved learning that I had what it takes to hike 2,200 miles.

To add to my experience, I decided to hike part of the Colorado Trail in 2018 – this time on a SOLO journey. It was the most empowering experience of my life. I learned that I could make it alone in the woods, that I could face my fears and, most importantly, that I could trust and rely on myself and that I am ENOUGH.

To any women out there considering to hike the AT – DO IT!

What was hardest thing about your hike?

During the early stages of our hike, we got rained on for almost three weeks straight. Having gear that was constantly wet and having to put on wet clothes in the morning (specifically underwear, socks, a sports bra for me, and moldy-smelling synthetic T-shirts) were probably our least favorite things about our hike.

Were there any sacrifices you had to make prior to pursuing your thru-hike?

Nothing felt like a sacrifice because whatever we did or sold or gave up prior to the hike enabled us to hike the AT. Prior to leaving the trail, we sold our second car, cut our belongings almost in half, and saved up as much money as we could, which meant no eating out, no additional trips, no buying new things, *etc.* None of this felt like a sacrifice though; it was a fun game we played. Justin called it "cheesburger economics." For every dollar we saved, we would be able to eat one extra cheeseburger while hiking. It made the entire saving experience fun and made us see hiking the AT as our great reward.

Did you have any fears or concerns before your hike? If so, how did you deal with them on trail, and how do you feel about them now?

I was terrified of sleeping in the woods, primarily because it was something I was not used to. We spent some time in the Alaska backwoods as well as thru-hiked the Foothills Trail to help me get used to that environment prior to our thru-hike, but I was still pretty scared when we first started. My fear quickly faded away, primarily because I was too tired to care about being scared and eventually learned that it was a lot more dangerous for me to go shopping at my local Walmart than it was to sleep out on trail.

To double-down, I went on an eight-day SOLO section hike of the Colorado Trail in 2018 to see if I felt as confident on trail alone as I had with Justin. It really helped me confront my fears and taught me that I am much more capable than I gave myself credit for. Today, sleeping in the woods with Justin or alone feels relaxing. Naturally I am always vigilant and make sure people know where I am or have bear spray with me when I am in Alaska, but it has given me a new level of confidence, and nowadays I get some of my best sleep when I am out in nature.

Did you have any post-trail depression? If so, how did you get through it?

I believe that hiking as a couple helped us ward off post-trail depression because we never truly left our trail community since Justin and I were each other's tramily. Additionally, we took a three-month vacation in Switzerland and weren't faced with the challenge of jumping from trail life straight into our old lives again. Having those three months helped us focus on the changes we wanted to put into place once we got back to Alaska and gave us time to digest our hike.

Finally, living in Alaska was probably the biggest reason why we did not experience post-trail depression. We are surrounded by rugged wilderness, and while we don't follow any white blazes up here, we spend every moment we can in the outdoors.

It is not realistic to be on the AT forever or to maintain that lifestyle. I think people can offset post-trail depression by having a plan and incorporating what the trail taught them into their post-trail life. For example, post-trail we moved into a smaller apartment, got rid of the majority our belongings, got involved in nature conservation, started following a plant-based diet, started to recycle and make what we can from scratch and spent every moment we could in the outdoors. We also went back to school to pursue jobs we actually love. We now invest our money in experiences rather than things, which has significantly enhanced our quality of life.

Do you view life differently in any way after hiking the trail?

We learned that people are inherently good and that the world isn't quite as dark as we were trained to believe. We enjoy the slower pace of life and invest in moments rather than things. I think the trail allowed us to gain an outsider's perspective. We see people rushing through life without really experiencing any of it, buying things to make up for a void because they are unhappy with life and capturing moments so they can post them on social media rather than being **in the moment** – that used to be OUR life as well. I think the trail helped us slow down and gave us the courage to blaze our own trail, to do things our own way and to take a step back from mainstream life. We learned that we can hike our own hike, even off trail.

If you could give your newbie hiker self any advice before starting the trail, what would it be?

• Don't send yourself resupply packages in advance. Whatever you are craving today will not be what you are craving by the time you pick up your package.

• Make sure you go to a running store prior to your hike and get fitted for proper trail runners.

• Don't believe everything people tell you – they are generally embellishing.

• You can never have too many baby wipes. Ever!

• Go on a shakedown hike prior to your thru-hike – it is an invaluable way to test your gear and to reduce pack-weight.

• Hike your own hike! (Or the saying I prefer: "Hike the way you like.")

What are your top tips or advice for women wanting to thru-hike the AT?

If the idea of hiking and sleeping alone in the woods terrifies you, it's a sure sign that you should DEFINITELY hike. While confronting your greatest fears might sound terrifying, overcoming them is that much more rewarding.

I was absolutely terrified of sleeping alone, and after spending six months on the AT and another eight days section-hiking the Colorado Trail SOLO, I can assure you that you will feel so much stronger after it all. Hiking SOLO was one of the most empowering things I have ever done. It showed me how strong I truly am and also confirmed that I am way more capable than I give myself credit for. This newfound strength and courage has positively impacted everything I do in my life off trail.

Anything else you'd like to mention?

Whether it be a thru-hike or section hike of any length on any trail, I believe every woman should go out into the wilderness on her own at some point in her life. It is hands down the most empowering experience I have ever had and has taught me that I am braver, stronger and more capable than I could have ever imagined.

Most of all, it taught me that I am enough – and I think that is something we could all benefit from learning, especially in a world where we are constantly told that we are not.

14. HANDSTAND (Liz Kidder)

Handstand started her 2018 thru-hike as a solo hiker. I first heard about her from *Evan's Backpacking Videos* on YouTube. Evan (E-Wolf) and Handstand had become a tramily and were hiking together. Upon first seeing Handstand, I was a bit intimidated by her – she has beautiful long dreadlocks and killer tattoos, and she was fit even in the beginning of her hike. What I didn't know right away was that she is an absolute sweetheart and a business owner, and she also has her own YouTube channel with amazing videos.

When I first reached out to her for help on my book, she immediately said *yes*, even though she was in the middle of her thru-hike at the time.

Web: www.lizkidderhair.com
Instagram: @LizKidder
YouTube: "Liz Kidder"

Tell me a bit about yourself.

I'm 30 years old and I live in Amesbury, Massachusetts. I thru-hiked in 2018, NOBO, and it took me took 161 days to complete (started 4/4 and ended 9/10).

How did you decide to hike the AT?

I never knew it existed until I was in my late 20s. A Facebook friend of mine hiked it and posted about it, and that's when I first learned of it. I did some more research and became obsessed with the idea. I had done a few day hikes before and had to know if thru-hiking was something I was capable of!

Did you hike the AT alone? Did you have a tramily at any point?

I went down to Georgia by myself to do it alone, although my (now) husband, Luke, had planned to come out and visit when he could. He ended up being able to come out more than we originally expected – he did about 1000 miles of the trail with me in total. He would come out and hike for two weeks, then go home and work for two weeks, and so on. I also made some friends on the trail, most importantly: Evan (E-Wolf). We met at the beginning of Virginia and hiked all the way to Katahdin together. We also hiked with Ricky (Yelp), mostly towards the end. It might be relevant to note that I am not a very social or extroverted person, nor do I drink or party, so I think other more social hikers tend to find a bigger tramily and find it earlier on.

Did you have any hiking or overnight camping experience before hiking the AT?

Only day-hiking. I had day-hiked 22 of New Hampshire's 48 4000-footers before heading out on the AT. I had zero camping or backpacking experience, but I did a lot of research and felt pretty prepared. I intended to get a short trip under my belt beforehand, but it didn't happen, and then I decided that I liked the extremeness of going in completely inexperienced. Not my recommendation for others – that's just my style.

Did you ever feel unsafe or threatened by a person, animal, or situation?

I was a little nervous with a couple of bear encounters, but it really wasn't anything that dramatic – more of a brief adrenaline rush. Then there was one middle-aged man that seemed mentally unstable and freaked out some people (he wasn't a thru-hiker; he just did a small section in Virginia), but I didn't feel personally threatened by him and I was around other people whenever I encountered him.

Did the AT change you? If so, how?

I'm still sort of figuring that out – I've been home for less than two months (at the time of writing this). I'm sure it did, but it's a gradual change that I'm starting to notice as I get back into my real life and look back on the experience. I think it made me stronger, mentally. I think it gave me a new sense of freedom and control over living a life that I want. I've always had those things, but the AT has amplified them. On a less significant note, I pack a lot less crap now when traveling somewhere.

Please explain the origin of your trail name.

Hand-balancing is a significant hobby of mine and has been since I was young. I have always done handstands at cool locations (traveling, mountain tops, *etc.*). A man called One Bearded Hippie dubbed me Handstand on my third day on the trail when I was doing a handstand on a summit. There were also two other Handstands on the trail this year that I know of, and I was fortunate to have had hand-balancing contests with both of thcm!

What was the most unexpected thing that happened or that you experienced?

I got Lyme Disease. We all know it's a risk, but no one thinks it will ever happen to them. Well, I guess it's more common than you would think – I met a few others who had gotten it before also. I got extremely sick; it was the most awful few weeks of my hike, but luckily we caught it early enough that they were able to treat it with medication and I should continue to be fine in the future.

Favorite hiker trash or funny moment?

We eat *a lot* of food out there. I refused to use privies, so I would go dig a hole in the woods. I also was lazy and would tend to hold it way longer than I should have. Getting into town, that was usually the first order of business I'd need to take care of. One motel we went to, I clogged the toilet right when I got there. I know, gross. I texted Evan and told him I would pay him five bucks to go to the front desk and get a plunger for me. He did. I tried and tried but could NOT unclog the toilet. I finally had to do the walk of shame to the front desk and let them know it was me and I needed help fixing it. They sent someone to the room; he tried for a few minutes and then said, "Oh ma'am, we're going to have to switch you to another room. I need a snake or somethin' to fix this! You definitely can't stay in here!" It was mortifying.

How was hiking the AT empowering for you as a woman?

I've always felt pretty empowered (or badass) as a woman, but I think by completing this trail, it's changed *other* people's perceptions of how capable I am, and I like that.

What was hardest thing about your hike?

Honestly, not a single thing stood out to me as extremely hard, but overall, the whole thing was somewhat harder than I thought it was going to be. As far as the physical difficulties – it's hiking. It was all doable, but nothing seemed particularly easy. I kept hearing or thinking that the next section of trail, whatever that was, was going to be easier than what I was doing currently, but it never was. Every section of the trail has its own challenges and difficulties for different reasons. Mentally, it was also harder than I thought. I've always been strong willed, but the trail gets monotonous after a while and the constant rain could make someone go crazy. The logistics and planning was also fairly hard – it was always a puzzle to be solved and tedious to figure out. Although, I'll admit, I am very Type A, so maybe most people don't put as much time and energy into that.

Were there any sacrifices you had to make prior to pursuing your thru-hike?

Before I left for my hike, I had owned my business, Liz Kidder Studio (a dreadlock studio), for 2.5 years. That was my biggest challenge. I left my friend and employee in charge of my studio while I was gone. She had to run the business and take care of all of my clients. It took *a lot* of preparation and planning beforehand, but it was well worth it, as I didn't have to oversee too much while I was away. Aside from that, I did give up my apartment and moved my stuff home temporarily so that I wouldn't have to pay rent while I was away.

Did you have any fears or concerns before your hike?

My only real fear or concern before my hike was that I might not finish it. I had been having some issues with a knee injury prior to the hike and was worried it might not hold up when trying to hike all day, every day. I did everything I could to prepare it beforehand (physical therapy, yoga, *etc.*), and luckily it paid off – my knee was not an issue on my hike.

What was your favorite trail food?

For dinner I liked a tortilla wrap with peanut butter, dried fruit and honey. For junk food, I liked gummy bears and Rice Krispies treats.

Did you have any post-trail depression? If so, how did you get through it?

Actually, yes, which I wasn't expecting at all since I was

really looking forward to coming home. I think I just got overwhelmed in real life because I was trying to catch up after the trip and go in a million directions at once. I missed (and still miss) the simplicity of the trail and being somewhat removed from the rest of society. Things are starting to settle down now though and I'm looking forward to a mini-trip we have coming up.

How did you feel on the day you finished your hike?

Of course, when I summited Katahdin and finished my hike, that was one of the most proud moments in my life. Some people get very emotional and cry or something – I didn't. I'm not a very emotional person anyway, and I think I had already been processing the fact that it was coming to an end for days and weeks leading up to that moment, so it wasn't a surprise or a rush of emotions.

I also had something else on my mind – and that was picking out a spot for my wedding ceremony! Luke and I had been planning to do this for a while and started making arrangements as we got closer to Katahdin. Evan got ordained, and we got off the trail in Maine to get our marriage license. On Summit Day, it was beautiful out! After we took some summit pictures and enjoyed the moment, we picked a spot to exchange our vows. There were about 20 other people up there – everyone was really respectful and quiet while we had our (very quick) ceremony, and then they all cheered when we were done! That was definitely the icing on the cake for this perfect day! I can't imagine my wedding happening any other way.

Do you view life differently in any way after hiking the trail?

I've always been fairly minimal in the way I try to live, but the AT has inspired me to take it to the next level. I've been obsessed with watching minimalism videos on YouTube and trying to downsize the amount of material things I have and to de-clutter my life in every possible way. I've donated about 75% of my wardrobe and a lot of other household items, but I still have a way to go on this journey. After living out of a backpack for five months, it became so clear to me that we *don't need* all this stuff!

If you could give your newbie hiker self any advice before starting the trail, what would it be?

There's nothing that I would go back and change or that I struggled with, so I guess I'd tell myself to chill the heck out! I obsess over everything and get super anxious about everything, and there wasn't a need for any of that. I got the hang of things as I went along and it all worked out fine!

What are your top tips or advice for women wanting to thru-hike the AT?

Do it! Girls are tougher than boys and we need more representation out there! Do your research first. Don't be scared to do it alone. Practice your bear bag throws before you go. Either be in a very secure relationship or don't be in one at all. Bring a menstrual cup and practice with it before you go.

15. SNUGGLES (Jessica Rakestraw)

Before we knew Snuggles, we knew her husband Darwin. We discovered his YouTube videos *Darwin onthetrail* when we were still living in Costa Rica and had just started thinking about the AT. Then all of a sudden, Darwin and Snuggles were out there ON the Appalachian Trail, and it was amazing following them. They were the first YouTube hikers we followed. We were thrilled and honored when they followed us on our thru-hike in 2017.

One of the many things I admire about Snuggles and Darwin is that they ditched their "real jobs" and figured out how to build enough income to support their adventurous lifestyle. Check out "The Snuggle Diaries" on their blog for Snuggles' take on their escapades.

Blog: darwinonthetrail.com/the-snuggle-diaries
Instagram: @the_snuggle_diaries

Tell me a bit about yourself: your age, where you live, when you hiked the AT, which direction, and how long did it take you?

My name is Jessica Rakestraw and my trail name is Snuggles. I am currently 32 years old and live full time out of a van. Technically, I guess that means I live anywhere and everywhere. I started my hike of the Appalachian Trail at the age of 29 in 2015 going northbound. Together my husband and I started our hike on March 10, 2015 and hiked until late July. We had to end our hike in Great Barrington, MA after over 1,500 miles due to multiple health complications (my husband contracted a tick-borne illness and had an infected tooth) along with a death in the family. We picked up our hike in early June of 2016 at the exact trailhead we left off. We continued northbound and summited Katahdin on July 22, 2016.

The six months we were off trail after our 2015 thru-hike attempt were the longest and most torturing months I have lived. The Appalachian Trail hung over our heads like a black cloud. Getting back on trail was all we could think about.

How did you decide to hike the AT?

The first time I remember hearing about the trail was via a documentary my husband and I watched about it and I thought it sounded awful. At the time I was still not 100% comfortable with backpacking, so the thought of spending months at a time in the woods seemed horrific.

A few years went by and we went back and forth with the

idea of moving to a different place. Both my husband and I had lived in our hometown our entire lives and found ourselves traveling more than living in our house.

After losing two very significant people in our lives within months of each other, it was like a tie was severed and we both felt collectively it was time for a change. I had really developed a love for backpacking by that time and done further research on the AT. The more I researched it, the more I wanted to do it. The AT suddenly became our sole focus.

We decided to sell everything we owned and travel out West (an area neither of us had been) for a month before starting a thru-hike of the AT. We figured the time traveling by van and on trail would allow us to explore other places and create ideas and options for what we wanted to do after our hike.

I know you hiked the AT with your husband. Tell me some positives and negatives regarding hiking with your spouse.

Before the AT, when we would take small hiking trips, we seemed to hike together a lot. These trips were, however, long weekend trips so we, of course, were hiking smaller miles. I guess you could say they were more mini-vacations for us to just get away. Darwin would occasionally hike ahead of me, but never too far.

During our first day out on the AT, this was also what I was expecting but was not the case. Darwin would hike out quite a bit ahead of me and then occasionally wait until we could at least wave to each other and then he would continue hiking. There was, of course, a ton of people out on the AT, so he knew I would always be around someone for safety. We would occasionally hike a few miles together, but his pace is so much faster than mine, I would be pushing myself to keep up, and in return, he would try to slow down for me, leaving us both uncomfortable.

We finally got to the point he would leave me notes or take a break long enough for me to catch up. We would check in with each other and he would take off again; we almost always spent lunch together. I went back and forth with how I felt about this. Sometimes (usually on a bad day, a tough climb or descent, *etc.*) I would be upset he wasn't with me, but in the same breath I would feel great, as I would accomplish these days, climbs, descents on my own!

Hiking more so on my own also allowed me to get to know other people, especially other women who were hiking. In 2015, we had a good trail family, so we would all bounce around hiking with each other, or when alone, it was good to know that just a little ahead was a hiker or just a little behind was another hiker.

In 2016, when we returned to the AT, our hike was very much a couple's hike and how I had expected our time to be in 2015. We seemed to hike a lot more together and made decisions more together. Before it was a mass group of people making decisions. In 2016, we had also started ahead of a majority of hikers, so there were fewer people on the trail to hike with, allowing us to depend on each other.

I loved the tramily and friends I had made on trail in 2015;

however, I also equally loved the friends I made on trail in 2016. Having to leave the AT made us appreciate the time we had out there the second time. We came back out with fresh legs and fresh minds. We knew more about what to expect and were more confident in ourselves. Not that it wasn't great the first time, but it felt like a gift to be out there again.

Did you have a tramily at any point?

Yes, we hiked several hundred miles with a majority of the same people. The people would hike ahead, hike slower, *etc.*, so we would be constantly bumping around with each other. We did, however, hike with one other hiker every day for over 1,500 miles. We hiked with Roub until maybe three weeks before we got off trail. We still keep in contact with most of our original tramily, especially with Roub. We also are still in contact with some good friends we made on trail in 2016.

Did you have any hiking or overnight camping experience before hiking the AT?

Yes, we did several backpacking trips prior to even deciding we wanted to hike the AT. Nothing crazy long, maybe two nights, possibly three? I originally hated camping, thanks to experiences I had in Girl Scouts. Darwin slowly started me out car camping, then we started backpacking. I hated it all at first, but slowly got more comfortable and grew to really love it.

Did you ever feel unsafe or threatened by a person, animal, or situation?

On the AT, no. Even as a woman on trail, I never had any issues with men (even when hiking alone). Most of the males I met ended up being more like brothers to me. Everyone in my experience treated each other as equals; the trail and the community around it doesn't care what your gender, race, or sexuality is. Everyone is out there to hike.

I do remember one camping trip, however, where raccoons started to invade our camp; they got a little too close for comfort.

Did the AT change you? If so, how?

Yes, it made me more aware of what I was capable of. I'm not afraid to try new things as much as I was before. The trail taught me that plans don't usually work but everything will pan out in the long run. I don't stress or worry about the unknown as much. I deal with situations as they come at me. I'm not afraid to ask for help and feel more open to the world around me where before I felt I was more sheltered.

Overall, I have a confidence that I never had before the AT. I don't see all people as bad or suspicious; the AT restored my faith in humanity.

Please explain the origin of your trail name.

I got my trail name within the first week. Darwin and I used trail names before the AT but decided to let the AT rename us. The first night on trail, I was nervous about falling out of the top bunk of a shelter to pee in the middle of the night, so I slept or snuggled next to the ladder along with another hiker who had the same worry. Darwin didn't even sleep next to me that night. The second night I ended up snuggling up to the same hiker as the night before and with Darwin. Couple days later around a campfire, I was cold and trying to snuggle with other hikers for warmth. It then came as a group decision I should be called Snuggles. I took the name in fear of getting something worse (Darwin had been trying to get another name stuck to me that was way embarrassing). I wanted something more badass but Snuggles stuck.

What was the most unexpected thing that happened or that you experienced?

Getting off trail in 2015. I remember specifically sitting around a hot tub with our tramily in Hiawassee, GA during our first zero day and talking about the statistics of finishing. We looked around the tub at each other and realized that at least two of us would not finish. Months later in Great Barrington, MA, Darwin and I thought of our friends in that tub. They were all still hiking; we were the two.

Favorite hiker trash or funny moment?

There is a ton but one that sticks out is falling down some rock steps coming down from Mt. Greylock. Darwin and I basically were done hiking for the day and taking a nero, and the town sidewalks were literally within sight. We were walking down these stone steps out of the woods and there was a lady out with her dog on a hike behind us. We were talking with her and I turned around to say something about her dog (it was a lab and reminded me of Bowie) when somehow I lost my footing, and my feet went out from under me. I tumbled down the hill and slammed my head on a tree. I was knocked silly and did my best not to cry as Darwin and the lady with her dog ran to check on me. I kept asking Darwin if I broke my glasses, even after he found them and told me no. I was like on repeat and couldn't stop asking him for some reason. I lay there for a little bit to get myself back to working order. I rose up my trekking pole and discovered it was super bent. That's when I started crying.

I ended up with a big goose egg on my forehead along with a nice looking scratch. You can see it in a few pictures and video taken afterwards. It's funny now and was even a little after the event, but I just couldn't stop asking about my glasses even when they were back on my face.

Favorite trail food?

Tuna packet mixed in with mac and cheese with cheese crackers (preferably Penguins) mixed in. I'm drooling just writing about it. The crunch of the crackers, the loads of cheese, the tang of the tuna... .

Did you have any injuries?

Surprisingly no. Besides a few blisters here and there, scratches, achy feet – nothing out of the ordinary, which is awesome because I tend to trip a lot and seem very accident prone.

How did you feel on the day you finished your hike?

Relieved. I smacked the Kathadin summit sign and felt relieved. That moment had lingered in our minds for over a year. It was in our minds when we started our hike in Georgia in 2015, when we left trail, during the months off trail, and then when we returned in 2016. It was this big piece of unfinished business that I felt I finally completed.

What was hardest thing about your hike?

Everything! The terrain, the mosquitos, my own body fighting against me, the extreme weather, my mental state, all of it. It is one of the hardest things I have ever done! I cussed and cried a LOT out on trail. But in the same way, it was also so rewarding and cleansing. I really pushed myself in ways I would never have done if I didn't hike it.

Were there any sacrifices you had to make prior to pursuing your thru-hike?

Totally! I gave up an amazing job that related to my degree. We gave up being comfortable and financially secure. I gave up quality time with my dog. I gave up quality time with my family, one of whom died two days after I got home in 2015. I gave up spending the last four months of her life with her. We gave up traveling a predictable path for an unknown, less traveled one.

Did you have any fears or concerns before your hike? If so, how did you deal with them on trail, and how do you feel about them now?

I was terrified of dealing with my period on the trail. Prior to the trail, I was having some real issues, which at one point landed me in the emergency room. I was terrified I would be out on trail and have a similar issue. There also didn't seem to be a lot of information on dealing with having a period on trail. I did find information but not exactly what I was looking for. Maybe I never would have due to my fear. Nothing I read would probably have been enough for me. I dealt with this by doing exactly what I did when not hiking. I didn't try anything new but kept up doing the things I was comfortable with. I used tampons and pads and continued taking regular pill-form birth control. The period was a total non-issue. I did, however, always carry a few tampons and pads with me regardless if I was on my period just in case. This made me feel comfortable and saved a few of my fellow ladies when they didn't have enough.

Did you have any post-trail depression? If so, how did you get through it?

I did, but probably more so when we got off trail early in 2015. I remember filing at the job I had and seeing names on files that were my friends' last names or names that somehow related back to the AT. We moved to Albuquerque, NM in 2015, so there was no one there we could talk to about trail life; no one even knew what it was. The long distance hiking community there is basically nonexistent, even though it is relatively close to the Continental Divide Trail (CDT). No one even knew what the CDT was.

In 2016 when we finally finished, it seemed easier for me to adjust. I missed the constant movement, but by then we had established some roots in Albuquerque, NM, so it was easier to become occupied and involved. Darwin was already making plans for another venture of some kind, and that area has tons of outdoor activities to offer. We seemed to both be looking forward to future adventures, not stuck in one we had left unfinished.

Tell us a bit about your current adventure.

After hiking the AT, I came to the conclusion I am more of a section hiker. I like to stop and enjoy areas and not have to always worry about mileage. Because of this and for the fact I just had no desire to hike the Pacific Crest Trail (PCT), I took the opportunity to drive the trail (while Darwin hiked it). I always had a hard time leaving trail towns on the AT; I wanted to spend more time there and explore, get to know the community, but when long-distance hiking, this is not an option. This, however, can be done when you have a van and choose not to hike!

As Darwin thru-hiked north on the PCT (2018), so did I along with our dog Bowie. I pulled off at trail towns here and there (there are not as many close towns to the PCT as you experience on the AT), and in some of the smaller ones have done trail magic such as cold beer, sodas, snacks, water, and, of course, lots of rides. This has allowed me interaction with hikers (I love to hear their stories) and gives me a small sense of the hiker life but without the hiking part.

Bowie and I also ventured off to do our own exploring at more roadside attractions: world's biggest rock, weird landscapes, odd town monuments, *etc.* We also, of course, hiked on smaller trails, not just little pieces of the PCT. Bowie can't hike as much due to her age but still enjoys the outdoors. I also took the opportunity to focus on my own projects, one of which was to put out a small book of my own and to write about my experiences traveling on my own. The whole experience was new to me as I have never fully lived on my own before. I have always had a roommate or lived with family or, of course, Darwin. This journey has been a new type of challenge for me.

Do you view life differently in any way after hiking the trail?

Yes, I know if I get stuck somewhere I can always hitch! Haha! I don't need to have the junk I thought I needed to live. We went from a two bedroom house to a studio apartment to a van plus a 5x8 cargo trailer to just a van. I never miss the stuff in our house – well maybe some of my books. I feel better with less stuff in my life. I'm also not afraid of the unknown – cautious, but not afraid.

If you could give your newbie hiker self any advice before starting the trail, what would it be?

Don't compare yourself to anyone else. Everyone is at different levels. Do what you can and what feels okay for your body. It's okay to bitch.

What are top tips or advice for women wanting to thru-hike the AT?

Don't let your lady parts define you or put limits on what you think you can do. You can do it!

16. KANGA (Bekah Quirin)

I knew about Bekah, Derrick and Ellie before we got on trail. Their story was online and in magazines everywhere as they were attempting an unusual thru-hike: they would be carrying their baby the whole way!

We ran into them at a swimming hole in Vermont. They had flipped up north at this point and were hiking southbound. They were having a hard day, but still took the time to chat with me. They were so friendly and unpretentious and Ellie was as happy as could be in the pack on her dad's back.

In 2018 they cycled the Great Divide Mountain Bike Route, which I watched unfold on Instagram (Sunsets and I are always thinking, *what's next?*). I had a delightful time chatting with Kanga (and Roo) for this interview.

Instagram: @thedirtbagbaby

Tell me a bit about yourself.

I was 25 when I started my AT thru-hike, and Ellie had just turned one. Two weeks after her first birthday, we started at McAfee Knob, VA, and hiked south to Georgia, then flipped to Maine and hiked south back to McAfee Knob. Derrick and I are very social and love being with people, so it was a bit hard doing a flip-flop hike because the first part of our hike went against the northbound bubble. Most hikers we saw were hiking the opposite direction. But once we flipped up to Maine, we were hiking with the southbound hikers, and we did meet and hike with many more people from this point on. It took us six months and ten days total, which included taking a month off in the middle of our hike for wedding and graduation stuff to do back home.

You chose to thru-hike the AT with your husband and baby, who turned out to be the youngest person ever to be carried on the AT as a thru-hike! Tell us about that decision and how you first decided to hike the AT.

Derrick and I had always dreamed of doing the AT, and we've always had a picture book of the Appalachian Trail on our coffee table. Before Ellie was born, my husband and I were outdoor guides and worked in a variety of different positions across the US. Outdoor trips, both week-long and day trips, were our passion and our fuel.

After Ellie was born, I was a stay-at-home mom. I felt the stereotype of "once you have a baby, those outdoor trips are over" – and definitely if you are breast-feeding. As I thought about it more after she was born, I started going on day hikes with her. She was six weeks old at the time. I noticed how natural it felt to be out with her, hiking in the woods. She seemed to be much more content, and I had so much more patience compared to running the rat race at home. We experienced a more natural flow when we were together outdoors. Derrick and I decided to do a couple of backpacking trips with Ellie to see how it would go. Well, everything was perfect, and we never wanted those trips to end!

We still hadn't talked about the AT at this point, so finally one day, I just came out and asked him, "What would you think about doing the AT with Ellie?"

He first said, "Are you serious?" But then it didn't take him long at all to say, "Well, sure, let's go for it!"

So we decided to commit to an AT thru-hike with Ellie but said we would go only as far as we were comfortable. We decided we would turn around or stop if we didn't feel safe or if we felt that we were putting her life at risk in any way. We made that commitment to one another, to our families, and to Ellie that our goal was not to finish but to do only as much as we could in the time we had.

It just so happened that we never felt uncomfortable having her with us on our hike. The days that weather and terrain were not safe (mainly the Whites in New Hampshire and parts of the trail in Maine), we'd take a break and not hike that day. I figured it was risky if there was a combination of two or more different things. With bad terrain by itself, we would simply take it really slow and be careful. Bad weather with easy terrain was the same – it sucked – but we would take long breaks in shelters or our tent.

Please explain the origins of your trail name (and your

husband's and Ellie's too).

I was Kanga and Ellie was Roo because she was in my backpack pouch like a kangaroo. Sherpa (Derrick) got his name from carrying all our extra stuff.

Did you experience any negativity from anyone before you started?

We chose to let our story be public and let the news cover our story. But because of this, we did get some online trolls that were not very kind. We still tried to listen to everyone, because a lot of these voices were out of genuine concern. We took them seriously, especially when they were telling us about certain sections of the trail that they thought would give us a hard time with a baby on our backs.

Other people were just hateful and mean, and we had to learn to put these comments out of our mind. This was hard to do at first, but after we got on the trail and became more confident, both as parents and hikers, we were able to take those hateful comments and not think about them anymore.

Did you have to have a lot of extra gear to hike with a baby?

Diapers were the biggest extra bulk. I had gone through the Awol's *Guide* and strategically found where we could resupply about every three to four days. I would contact them, make sure we could have a box sent there, and we would send the minimum number of diapers I'd need for Ellie. She needed four diapers per day, and we tried to carry only 12-16 diapers at a time. We had to stick to an itinerary and it worked well.

We had a lot of trash, especially from the diapers. The diapers were compostable, but it would have taken us longer to dig a hole and bury them than to just carry out the trash. We went above and beyond to try to find trashcans. Several day hikers offered to hike our trash out for us, which was really kind, but we also wouldn't hesitate to ask people as well. The biggest thing for us was sticking to our itinerary so we didn't have to carry a ton of extra trash.

As far as our packs went, we had one pack that was also a carrier for Ellie. I started out carrying Ellie the first 800 miles, but after the 100-mile wilderness, we got rid of our winter gear. All the gear left was lighter than Ellie, so because Derrick wanted to carry the heavier pack, which was Ellie at that point, we switched.

Did you ever feel unsafe or threatened by a person, animal, or situation?

No, never.

Did the AT change you? If so, how?

It made me a very adaptable human being and a very adaptable mom. I can live anywhere now and be in any environment and be calm, relaxed, and comfortable. I gained a sense of peacefulness from the whole experience. On the AT you are constantly adapting to the weather and the terrain, so that definitely transitioned into my life now. Before the AT I had to stick to my schedule. And if anything was different I might work myself into a tizzy. Now, people can throw last minute things at me or randomly change my schedule and I'm totally cool with it.

Any bad experiences on the AT?

My least favorite moment was when we got kicked out of a hostel. We had a reservation for a private room in New Hampshire. But as soon as they saw me with Ellie, and realized she was a baby who would be staying for the night, they said, "Oh, you have a baby with you? We can't have you stay here. She'll disturb the communal atmosphere of the hikers." Even though we told them we were in a private room, not the bunkroom, and that we would keep Ellie in our room, it didn't matter to them. They said it was one of their policies on their website, which I looked up later and found no such policy at all. The sun was setting, and there were no other accommodations within walking distance. But a hiker who had come by and had seen what was going on invited us to join him and his family at a campsite down the road, which was super nice. So it ended up working out, but for a while it was not fun and to this day leaves me with a bad memory.

How did you feel on the day you finished your hike?

It was a bittersweet moment because our bodies were ready to be done. We were very tired and suffering the typical things thru-hikers deal with: everything was hurting. We had seriously pushed the last several miles, and Derrick was dealing with plantar fasciitis as well. Mentally and emotionally it was also hard: we knew that, as soon as we finished, we were going back to work and would no longer be in our intimate family setting on the trail anymore. We were very excited to finish but also sad to know that things weren't going to be the same anymore. The good thing was that it motivated us to plan more trips for the future.

McAfee Knob was the end for us, as well as near where we lived, so we had lots of family waiting for us. They were all there at the top of McAfee, so to see them all there at our finish was amazing. They had been our support throughout the whole trip, and it meant so much for them to be there for us at the end.

How was hiking the AT empowering for you as a woman?

As a woman, it gave me a sense of hope and rejuvenation for women to have an equal role in the outdoors. Every hiker, regardless of gender, seems to be an equal in the woods with equal responsibilities and equal expectations. I realized that I, as a woman, am capable of doing hard tasks and that it is acceptable for me to do those hard tasks. I love that there are more and more women on the trail than ever before.

Having Ellie on the AT with me felt normal. It wasn't a magical or super-mom feeling. It just felt like that's where I was supposed to be, and that's where Ellie was supposed to be at that time in our lives. It's where we belonged.

What was hardest thing about your hike?

Ellie would sleep or relax in her carrier while we were hiking, but when it was time for us to take a break from hiking, that's when she would want to get out and explore and run around (she learned to walk on the AT). Of course, we had to watch her all the time, so I felt I could never relax and turn off my brain. This was definitely the hardest part for me.

About halfway through our hike, Derrick and I finally

figured out of a schedule, and we started taking turns. One person would watch Ellie while the other would rest or sleep for 30 minutes, which worked out great but wasn't always feasible.

Did you have any fears or concerns before your hike?

Weather in the Whites was the biggest thing I was concerned about. I was terrified of being in an exposed environment, unable to escape lightning storms with Ellie. It hung over my head the entire time. There did end up being a big storm in New Hampshire, but we knew it was coming so we took off for three days and waited it out.

I was also nervous about the 100-mile wilderness. More than anything, I just didn't know what to expect. Once I was out there, I was fine. There were old forestry service roads where someone could get in or out of the woods if something happened.

If you could give your newbie hiker self any advice before starting the trail, what would it be?

Don't work yourself up over little things. Take things more day by day. Once you get onto the trail, it won't be as stressful as you expect it to be.

Never make a rash decision on a hard day, especially when you feel low emotionally, because chances are you'll wake up the next morning with a different attitude.

What are your top tips or advice for women wanting to thru-hike the AT?

If you're worried about being alone at night, don't be. Unless you stealth camp, you'll probably never be alone at night on the AT. It's a very social trail if you want it to be. You can definitely build a community of people. You can hold each other accountable and support one another.

Be confident in your decisions. If you decide to hike the AT, you're not going to go out and do it the next day – you prepare for months (hopefully). And you need not only physical training and gear preparation, but also mental and emotional preparation. You made the decision to hike the AT, so be confident and proud of yourself, and just go for it!

Did you have any post-trail depression? If so, how did you get through it?

I thought I was fine, but in retrospect, I actually went into a mini-depression over the winter after our thru-hike. I didn't recognize it at the time, but now that I'm out of it, I can definitely see that it was a low spot.

We just recently finished our 2,760-mile bike adventure, the Great Divide Mountain Bike Route, from Canada to Mexico. This time I know what to expect, so I have taken some preventative measures like making sure I have things on the calendar to look forward to, including getting outside more.

Tell me a bit about your recent cycling trip.

It was amazing. I loved it probably more so than Derrick, as he was sick for almost half of it. He got some kind of parasite, stomach, or intestinal issues for six out of the nine weeks. I had a stomach bug for three days but then was fine. He could never kick it.

The part of the country we cycled through was beautiful, but it's different from the AT. For days at a time, you're looking at the exact same thing, and you don't have the twists and turns like you do on the AT where you're always seeing new things. On the bikes, we were looking at the same giant mountain that was 50 miles ahead *all day long*. I grew in areas that I didn't have much experience in with the bike. And, of course, we enjoy spending time with Ellie, so it was great.

Any adventures planned for the future?

Right now, we are rebuilding our savings and living with my in-laws. We are sort of in limbo-land with Ellie as she's at the stage where she's too big and independent to want to be carried all the time, but also too young and small to travel long distances by herself. My parents have bought some land near Dragon's Tooth, VA. It's a mile and a half from the AT and the Trans-America Bike Route, and our plan is to build a home and seasonal hostel for hikers and cyclists.

We will take it easy and do some shorter trips until Ellie has the ability and desire to do stuff on her own; we need to keep her desires in mind. Maybe the Mississippi River at some point? Ellie doesn't need too much stamina for it, and she can paddle as much or as little as she wants.

Sometimes it's hard to believe we really did the whole AT, but then I think about all the amazing moments and also all the hard times, and I think, *Yep, that was real.*

17. TENACIOUS (Erin Bogert)

The first time I remember seeing Tenacious was at Standing Bear Hostel after we hiked through some rainy days in the Smokies. A bunch of us were on the porch taking shelter from the rain, and we were taking turns stepping on the scale to see how much weight we'd lost. I immediately knew I liked Tenacious when she stepped on the scale proclaiming, "I don't care if I've lost weight or not, I'm fine with myself how I am!"

Later, we were at Doe River Hostel together, all of us taking a zero day, when we indulged in my éclairs and she let me interview her for our YouTube channel.

Tenacious was a solo hiker, very tenacious (ha), and just plain fun to hang with.

Tell me a bit about yourself.

I live in Connecticut and I turned 35 years old on my thru-hike in 2017. I was a NOBO (Northbounder), and it took me six months to complete the trail.

How did you decide to hike the AT?

I had spent the past few years trying to get fit, and hiking played a huge part in that. I had day-hiked all over the place with my sister, and hiking made me happier than anything else. I was working a job that was wearing me down and making me really unhappy, and I knew it was time for a change and also a new challenge. I felt drawn to the AT, and I thought to myself, why not? I don't have kids. I don't have a house to take care of. I'm free to go. So I saved up for about a year, moved out of my apartment, quit my job, and went. It just seemed like the right thing to do at the time.

Did you hike the AT alone? Did you leave family, and how did you cope with missing them? Did you have a tramily at any point?

I hiked alone, but as many people will say, you are rarely totally alone out there. I had a trail sister named Nighthawk who I camped with almost every night, and another trail sister named Noon Noodle with whom we were on pace for several states. I loved having someone to camp with at night, but preferred to go at my own pace and be alone during the day. There were a few days of bad weather or tough terrain when we decided it would be safer to hike together.

I have the most wonderful and supportive family at home

and I love them so much. They even drove me to Springer Mountain and picked me up in Millinocket – that's how amazingly supportive they are. So, it might sound strange to say that I didn't miss them on the hike, but I didn't. I called home from time to time and even met up with them a couple times when I was up North. I was, of course, very happy to see them after the trail as well. But I was out there to make a change and try something new, and I just embraced the experience and people of the trail; I was focused on the path in front of me. I actually feel closer to my family now after returning from the hike. And I think having a tramily that you can count on plays a huge part in feeling at home on the trail.

My trail sisters and I are still in touch and hike together whenever we can. You really do form a lasting bond working through challenging situations together, supporting each other on tough days, sharing motels, laundry, and putting up with each other's stench.

Did you have any hiking or overnight camping experience before hiking the AT?

Just one night of backpacking! And it wasn't even in my tent! I had stayed overnight at the RMC Grey Knob hut in the Presidential Range of the Whites. Otherwise, I had just car camped. Backpacking was very much a learning process on the AT. I think back to my first couple of nights on trail and laugh at myself. I guess you could say I'm a very all-or-nothing type of person.

Did you ever feel unsafe or threatened by a person, animal, or situation?

For the most part, I never felt unsafe, save for one or two sketchy guys at trailheads or shelters. Hikers tend to be a friendly and honest bunch of people, and we all looked out for each other. There were a couple bear encounters that made my heart skip a beat, but that was about it. And just FYI, bears do not always run away from you if you're only five feet tall!

Did the AT change you? If so, how?

The AT opened my mind to more possibilities. I'm less fearful of things in general, but I wouldn't call myself brave. It gave me new perspective about what matters and what counts as a real problem.

Please explain the origin of your trail name.

My trail name is Tenacious. The first few days in Georgia, I got horrible blisters that turned my heels into hamburger for weeks. I taped them up with moleskin and wrapped bandages around my ankles and kept walking.

What was the most unexpected thing that happened or that you experienced?

I was blown away by the kindness of complete strangers and the trust in the trail community. So many people helped me out when I was hurting with the blisters, and later Achilles tendonitis. I was completely overwhelmed by people's generosity and genuine concern. There were so many kindhearted and down-to-earth hikers, trail angels, and people in trail towns. The AT would not be the same without them. People invite you into their homes, give you food, rides to resupply, expecting nothing in return. It still amazes me. I never felt I deserved such kindness just because I was walking a trail.

Favorite hiker trash or funny moment?

It's hard to pick one – there were so many – but I distinctly remember sliding down a ravine in the Smokies on my bare bottom with my pants around my ankles during a bathroom and bug incident. That's probably enough detail.

Favorite trail food?

Swedish Fish.

How did you feel on the day you finished your hike?

On the day I finished my hike, I actually didn't feel all that much. I hiked up to the Katahdin sign and was like, *well, I guess this is it. I guess it's over.* I felt fortunate, grateful, acutely aware that much of my being there was beyond my doing or control. I had been hiking towards this for months, so I had expected a much more emotional reaction. My head knew that I had finally reached the finish line, but emotionally it didn't register. When I went down to the hostel in Millinocket, I was glad I had reserved a single room. I wanted to be alone for a bit. I felt quiet.

I'm sure part of this is due to the fact that I knew I still had a few days to make up in New Jersey and New York from when I was injured. I made up the miles the following week. But when I finished there, the feeling remained the same.

How was hiking the AT empowering for you as a woman?

It was empowering in so many ways. I was out there doing things that I was afraid of. And there were so many other women out there doing it, too! Nighthawk was 18, had graduated high school early to hike the trail and headed out solo. I met a section hiker in Maine in her 70s who was completing the AT for the third time. I was amazed by all these women on the trail holding their own, getting through tough conditions while keeping their humor and supporting each other. It was really refreshing.

What was hardest thing about your hike?

The endless rain in May was tough! But I reminded myself that it was so much better than being at work. There was also the physical pain of the Achilles tendonitis and the doubt that it cast over my hike. I kept wondering if I was going to make it and decided that I would just keep hiking as long as my body would let me, to take it as it came. It wasn't easy to come to terms with the fact that much of what happened out there was beyond my control.

What about your injuries?

As mentioned, I had bad blisters in the beginning and Achilles tendonitis in my left heel. It started late in Virginia and got increasingly worse until Killington, Vermont, when I finally tried some new shoes. That helped a lot. I also did a lot of stretching, wore ankle braces, and probably took more ibuprofen than I should have.

Were there any sacrifices you had to make prior to pursuing your thru-hike?

I gave up cable TV, eating out, anything to help save money. I think giving up some luxuries also helped mentally prepare for the trail.

Did you have any fears or concerns before your hike? If so, how did you deal with them on trail, and how do you feel about them now?

Ummm, bears, bears, and bears. I'm definitely less afraid after hiking by several of them. They didn't care much about my presence. I still take all of the precautions I should with my food, but otherwise I don't worry too much.

I never did end up camping alone on the AT. I'm sure I will end up doing it at some point, but I feel better camping with another person and have more fun with a friend anyhow.

Did you have any post-trail depression? If so, how did you get through it?

Yes. I'm still getting through it; I've missed the trail so much this year (the year after I hiked the trail). Staying in touch with trail friends has helped a lot as has joining hiking groups online. I find I need to get out to the woods as much as possible to stay even somewhat balanced. I'm still trying to figure out how to find that balance moving forward. It's a work in progress.

Do you view life differently in any way now, after hiking the trail?

I value time much more now – having the time to do what I love and spending time with people. Also, I find that I am much more inspired to learn new things, acquire new skills. I want to learn how to be more self-sufficient.

If you could give your newbie hiker self any advice before starting the trail, what would it be?

It's going to be all right. Trust in God. He will look out for you in more ways than you can imagine.

What are your top tips or advice for women wanting to thru-hike the AT?

My advice to other women would be to get out and do it. Don't regret not taking the chance.

Leave your expectations at the trailhead. Many things will not be at all what you expected, but some will be better. Just go with the flow.

Also, pee rags are an amazing piece of gear and getting an Ursack will completely change your hike for the better. Having to hang your food after a long day of hiking becomes a real pain after a few hundred miles.

18. KARMA (Nichole Fortier Young)

Karma solo thru-hiked the AT in 2016, the year before I did, and I followed her on Instagram. She hiked fast and I was amazed to see her posts fly by. Afterwards, she was very kind to help me with questions I had about odd things (like how do you brush your teeth in the woods?). She has gone on to do other amazing hikes as well as guided hikes for women on the West Coast.

Instagram: @nicholeyoung1

Tell me a bit about yourself.

I am originally from NJ but moved to the Bay Area in California last year, and hiked NOBO in 2016 when I was 30 years old. It took 151 days (or just shy of 5 months), from April 25 to September 22.

How did you decide to hike the AT?

I had been introduced to backpacking in 2013 when a friend organized a three-day trip through Zion National Park for a group of us who had never backpacked before. We made so many rookie mistakes on that first trip, but we were all hooked. I fell in love with backpacking on that original trip in 2013 and looked around for the biggest and baddest backpacking trip there was – and found the Appalachian Trail. My friend, although well meaning, told me he didn't think it would be safe for me to thru-hike alone as a woman, and I accepted his opinion since he had much more experience than I did. However, I started doing my own research and seeking out information from other women who had thru-hiked successfully. We went again with that same group in 2014 (Teton Crest Trail) and 2015 (Yosemite). By 2016 I felt ready to take on the AT solo.

Did you hike the AT alone? Did you leave family, and how did you cope with missing them? Did you have a tramily at any point?

I started alone and had no intention of finding a trail family – I didn't want to end up adjusting my hike for other people I'd just met. But on my very first night out, I met four other people who I clicked with. Without trying, we just ended up being on each others' wavelengths with pace and distance and planning, and I ended up summitting Katahdin five months later with three of them.

The hardest part of my hike was leaving my husband behind. We had only gotten married six months before I started, and although he was wonderful and supportive, he had no interest in backpacking. He was perfectly happy staying home and holding down the fort there, but it was hard being apart and taking on that big adventure without him. We were only able to see each other four times in five months – he came to visit me on trail twice and I went home twice. I couldn't have done it without him cheering me on and supporting me.

Did you ever feel unsafe or threatened by a person, animal, or situation?

Actually, my scariest, most unsafe moment was due to weather, not animals or people. It was on a double-peaked mountain in Maine before the Hundred Mile Wilderness. A storm was whipping up, and I was hiking fast to try to summit both of these little peaks and get down. I got over the first hump, descended into the dip, and started climbing the second peak when I saw lightning. By now I was above tree line, all alone, and the wind was raging – it was ripping my poncho almost off my body – and it was raining, but the rain was being blown around and the wind was so strong that I could hardly see and could barely walk in a straight line. I had no idea how much farther I had to go in these exposed conditions. I was close to panicking. *Do I go back and hunker down for who knows how long? Do I stop in place and get low to avoid a lightning strike? Do I push on and risk being even more exposed but maybe eventually descend?* It's the closest I ever came to crying on the AT, but I kept reminding myself that crying wouldn't solve anything and would only make it harder to see. I chose to keep moving forward one step at a time and eventually made it through and got back below tree line, but it felt like a truly dangerous situation that I was lucky to get through safely.

Did the AT change you? If so, how?

I think it did change me in subtle ways. I am calmer in stressful situations, partially because most of my day-to-day situations now aren't truly dangerous in the way a storm above tree line is, so it's given me perspective. I am also more confident in myself and know that, if I'm persistent, I can do pretty much anything.

Please explain the origin of your trail name.

My trail name comes from creating good karma while on trail. I'm a yoga teacher, and often in the evenings at the shelters, I would teach a mini hiker's yoga class for whoever was around. I also used my hike as a fundraiser and raised almost $3,000 for clean water through water.org.

What was the most unexpected thing that happened or that you experienced?

This might be odd, but maybe the most unexpected thing that happened to me during my thru-hike was that I became a feminist. Maybe I'm sheltered or lucky or oblivious, but being on the AT was the first time I remember experiencing blatant sexism. I guess since I'd never dealt with it firsthand, I'd never given much thought to how women are so often treated as less capable, but it became obvious in the semi-wild AT experience. I regularly encountered men who tried to tell me how to do things that I'd been doing successfully my own way for months. I had a woman in Massachusetts tell me I was lucky I had some big strong men around me to protect me. A man hiking in jeans(!) in Maine tried to tell me

I was too cute to have hiked all the way there from Georgia. People constantly asked me if my husband had given me permission to go hiking or if he was paying for my hike (I worked five jobs to save for my hike). Once I noticed it, this questioning and doubting was everywhere, and although I was shocked at first, I now channel my frustration into being a positive voice, encouraging more girls and women to get outside, to learn hiking and backpacking basics, and to never doubt themselves just because someone questions a woman being in the wild.

Favorite hiker trash or funny moment?

One of my favorite hiker trash stories happened to two friends in the town of Rangeley, Maine. The trail is a good 10-minute ride outside of town, so most people try to hitch in or out. My friends were walking away from town and toward the trail, unsuccessfully trying to catch a ride. Finally, a pick-up truck passed them, then pulled over in front of them to the shoulder. They ran up, threw the packs in the bed, and opened the door to the cabin, thanking the driver profusely. The driver looked at them in shock and annoyance.

"No, you misunderstood. This is my house. I live here."

My mortified friends apologized profusely and had to retrieve their packs from the truck belonging to an innocent resident who was just trying to park outside his house.

Favorite trail food?

Peanut butter M&Ms. Despite being an ultralight hiker, by the end of my hike, I was carrying a two-pound bag of peanut butter M&Ms. The saddest part was when opening the bag, I ripped the top off and M&Ms went flying everywhere on the trail and the ground. You better believe I picked up every single M&M off the ground and ate them all. I guess that's also pretty hiker-trashy!

Did you have any injuries?

Nothing acute, but I went through the whole range of typical hiker pains: massive blisters, losing skin off my feet, and achy knees, ankles, hips, back, feet, *etc.* It took about a month after my hike ended before I could get out of bed in the morning without hobbling and limping, and about six months until my knees started to feel normal again.

How did you feel on the day you finished your hike?

It took a while to sink in so I didn't feel any different! My husband met me up in Maine and we spent some time in Bar Harbor and Acadia, so it was a good transition period. However, what does stick out is that, on the way back down Katahdin, some day-hikers asked if we were thru-hikers. It was shocking when we realized, "Not anymore!"

How was hiking the AT empowering for you as a woman?

It made me feel so much more confident and badass! I don't politely smile and laugh when people make ignorant and sexist comments but try to call out sexism and misogyny when I see it now. Especially as a petite, not-athletic woman, doing something so physically demanding was especially empowering.

What was hardest thing about your hike?

Being away from my husband and my family. Life was going on as normal back at home, and my husband was amazing and held down the fort like a champ, but knowing I was missing our day-to-day life and that I could, in theory, go back to it at any time was a struggle.

Did you have any fears or concerns before your hike? If so, how did you deal with them on trail, and how do you feel about them now?

My biggest fear was that I would miss home and my husband too much to finish and wouldn't make any friends or have anything in common with the other hikers. Luckily, although I missed him very much, we got through it and our relationship is stronger than ever, and I made some great friends and had a blast hanging out with fellow thru-hikers.

Did you have any post-trail depression? If so, how did you get through it?

Yes! It didn't hit for a few months, so I started to doubt it was real. I stayed on a great post-hike high until the following January, but then it hit hard – maybe it was seeing other people getting ready for their own thru-hikes and knowing mine was over, or maybe it was that I didn't know what I was going to do with my own life post-trail and was feeling a little lost. After achieving such a big goal, I know it's normal to feel down, so I started planning my next hiking trip. I spent some time on the Long Trail in Vermont and the John Muir Trail, moved to California and started a new job that I love, and now I focus on finding awesome weekend trips and exploring a new state with my husband and our new dog.

Do you view life differently in any way after hiking the trail?

I like to think I'm more confident and more willing to take on adventures!

If you could give your newbie hiker self any advice before starting the trail, what would it be?

Stay calm, enjoy every day, don't overthink, and trust that you're capable.

What are your top tips or advice for women wanting to thru-hike the AT?

Hiking the AT is incredibly difficult and it shouldn't be undertaken lightly. However, if you do your research and preparation, make good decisions, and keep moving forward one day at a time, you'll be able to thru-hike. It's not easy, but it's simple.

Anything else you'd like to mention?

So many people are so scared before they start that they won't be able to finish. But everyone I know who quit the AT did so because they had gotten everything they needed out of it – they chose to leave and were at peace with their decision. Some have gone back to finish after a year or two, but some have never returned and they're perfectly happy. So don't obsess over finishing 2,200 miles. Enjoy the journey!

19. HONEYBEE (Deborah Griffin)

I first met HoneyBee during a trail-magic break on our hike. While munching on Girl Scout cookies and potato chips, she told me about the recent loss of her parents and how she was hiking for them as well as raising money and awareness for Alzheimer's. I was struck by her story, her openness and her passion for life and hiking.

Email: debgriffin@thegriffinslair.com

Tell me a bit about yourself.

I am a 50-year-old, non-professional, multi-sport athlete who has many distractions in life. I'm a wife, a mom, a business owner, a volunteer and a fundraiser. I am from the south shore of Massachusetts. I hiked the AT northbound in 2017 (as well as a long section in 2016).

How did you decide to hike the AT? I know you had recently lost both of your parents. Did this affect your

decision at all?

I returned to hiking when both my parents were battling Alzheimer's disease. They had it simultaneously. It was the most difficult and challenging part of my life. Keep in mind, my husband had battled stage four throat cancer just a few years prior to my parents' decline. My mom was diagnosed back in 2002. She had a long journey with her disease, true Alzheimer's. My dad was diagnosed in 2012 with frontotemporal dementia. To say that it was a difficult journey is an understatement. For the last four years of their lives, they lived in a memory-care residence. They were able to share a room. This was the most important aspect of their care to me, that they remain together. They had been together since the age of 14, life partners in everything they did. The GREATEST love story ever. I am an adopted child, truly wanted by them, and more than blessed to have had them as my parents. I could not have hand-picked two better people to raise me, teach me values and integrity, and show and share with me a lifetime of love. All they blessed me with served as motivation for their care.

Many days ended with my face in my hands sobbing as I watched them lose little pieces of themselves every day. No matter what the disease stole from them, my mantra was that "the love remains." No matter what memories were robbed from their minds, they always loved me and knew that there was a bond. Even on the days they could no longer remember my name and eventually when they could no longer speak, I could always see the love and trust in their eyes. My commitment to them never waivered, but all that care for two people on a daily basis took a toll on me.

I had cared for and nursed and nurtured my parents through the end stages of their disease from 2012 through 2015, then they both passed. My mother left us in January and my father left in November. I turned my self-therapy hikes into fundraisers. I planned a long-distance hike to honor my parents and raise money for the Alzheimer's Association. In 2016 I hiked Massachusetts, Vermont and New Hampshire in totality and the southernmost portion of Maine.

I hiked. A lot. It became my therapy. As those day hikes turned to overnights, turned to weekends, and finally my LASH (Long Ass Section Hike) in 2016, I dreamed of an AT thru-hike, but thought it best to test myself by hiking the region I knew best as a test of my skills and will to complete a long-distance hike. I hiked those New England miles and it was empowering. I thrived as I climbed my beloved summits in the Whites and earned my "badass badge." I hiked solo. I had a couple friends join me here and there for a few days, but it was mostly a solo effort.

I immediately began to plan and prepare for my 2017 thru-hike attempt. I was in need of a full and thorough healing. Georgia is where I would begin.

Did you hike the AT alone? Did you leave family, and how did you cope with missing them? Did you have a tramily at any point?

I did hike solo, no friends joining this time around. I, of course, made friends and developed a trail family. I hiked the first 300 miles with my hiking friend, Tina from Montana (T-Squared). And at Uncle Johnny's, I began hiking with Dove. Amber (her real name) was from Georgia.

We were a great fit as hiking partners. Happy to hike miles together and solo and always meeting up at camp. There were other trail family members: Prism and her dog Scout, Punz, Fresh and Bean, Ironman and Tin Man, Young Gandalf, Patch, Jimmychanga, Captain No Beard, Mammoth, Y'all, The Maine Sisters, Many Miles, 99, 7, 12, Bambi, Second Dinner, Witch Doctor, Sunshine, Dollar, Pogo, Quincy, Wilson, McGyver, Marshmallow and, of course, Chica and Sunsets! The list could literally go on for pages!

Did you have any hiking or overnight camping experience before hiking the AT?

Yes, plenty. Lots of camping and hiking when I was young. Saco River trips, White Mountain National Forest, Maine and Cadillac Mountain. And I prepared by doing sections and building confidence in the White Mountains. I felt pretty well prepared when I began my thru attempt.

Did you ever feel unsafe or threatened by a person, animal, or situation?

Only once. Dove and I had hitched to a church for a shower and overnight dry place to sleep. We got a ride from a guy who said he was a section hiker. At first he appeared that way, but his gear was really new and clean. We made it to the church OK but the next day he appeared on trail and followed us. Said he was there specifically to see us. Totally creepy. Asked me if I was carrying any weapons. Wanted to know if Dove had any weapons. Thankfully, we were able to get away from him and double time it up the trail to the safety of a shelter with plenty of trail family waiting to remind us we were not alone.

Did the AT change you? If so, how?

Loaded Question. Yes, I was changed in so many ways. I feel like there is nothing I can't do but realize the fragility of life at the same time. I have no fear of going to places unknown or travelling alone as long as I'm prepared. I have a healthy dose of caution and good judgment to carry me through the rest of my days. I don't feel invincible; I feel very strong and confident in my abilities. I know my limitations and would only push beyond them with assistance or guidance. But the world is a very big place, and the woods gave me the opportunity to look inside myself as well as to take in the world around me. Little things hardly bother me. I am saddened by how mean people are to one another in the world at large; hikers are such good people. I can't really watch the news since returning form the trail – too depressing. And not a day goes by that I don't long to be a long-distance hiker again. I cherish my outdoor time now that I'm back in an office. Every. Single. Minute.

Please explain the origin of your trail name.

I'm adopted. My birth parents had me baptized with the name Pamela. In Greek it means "all honey." My adoptive parents named me Deborah; in Hebrew it means "bee." My hiking friend Immrum named me HoneyBee.

What was the most unexpected thing that happened or that you experienced?

I discovered I'm completely self sufficient and that my loved ones are as well. It was an unexpected part of the journey.

Understanding that my life moved forward in a parallel place to theirs, not touching for five and a half months. Strange because I missed them but I found myself growing stronger and more independent. I have absolute faith in my ability to care for myself. Yet, I crave to be loved by my family and friends. A strange juxtaposition but empowering at the same time.

Favorite hiker trash or funny moment?

Swimming in my underwear or skinny-dipping, knowing I could light a fire in the rain.

Favorite trail food?

Peanut butter and Nutella on Honey Stinger waffles; my meals were great because I made them all, dehydrated and vacuum-sealed them, and had my husband send to me once a week. I ate really well. Favorite candy was sour gummies. In fact, I'd ration them to myself so I'd be able to have some every day for dessert.

Did you have any injuries?

Ugggh, yes. I herniated my L4-L5 disc and had frozen piriformis syndrome. The injury took me off trail after I had jumped to Maine to hike southbound. I had gotten a call from my physician after I solo hiked and summited Katahdin. I was almost in the 100-Mile Wilderness and had to get off trail.

How did you feel on the day you finished your hike?

Sad. I was so comfortable on trail and with trail life. Going back to the noise of everyday life was disconcerting. I found people to be very mean in general and have very little patience. It was an adjustment to everything in everyday life when I returned home. Re-entry was a bit difficult. Hikers are so kind.

How was hiking the AT empowering for you as a woman?

ABSOLUTELY! Can't wait for my next solo adventure. I'm healing nicely and thinking about what that will look like.

Did you have any fears or concerns before your hike? If so, how did you deal with them on trail, and how do you feel about them now?

Fear of leaving my husband for such an extended period of time. He didn't visit with me on trail and it was difficult to be away. We spoke each day by phone or text, but it is no replacement for seeing one another. The hike changed me in so many ways. I became so independent and yet I missed my husband so much. He carried on. He missed me, but I think I was surprised to find out that when I got home he just carried on in an independent way by himself. We had to find our way back to one another on some levels. We loved one another through the separation, but the distance definitely changed the tone of our relationship. It was hard for me when I realized that my absence impacted him less than it did me. Still love, but it was somehow… different at first.

Did you have any post-trail depression? If so, how did you get through it?

YES! Thankfully I was able to return to my business walking dogs and being out in the woods each day. I eventually returned to real estate, but had I gone right to that from the trail, it would not have gone well. The woods at home gave me a buffer for the trail and back into the real world. I spent a lot of time on my own and continued to work on myself as an extension of my hike. I had to develop a new skill set to re-enter the life I left behind.

Do you view life differently in any way after hiking the trail?

Many things that I used to worry about no longer matter, and conversely, there are new things that mean so much to me. You can't walk over 1,700 miles in the woods and not change. It's a mental shift as much as an emotional one. I think of my days on trail fondly – a treasure that belongs just to me. A transformation of part of me into a badass that fears nothing. I am far more able to "roll with it," and my long-term goals are very different. I want to travel and see as much of the world as possible.

If you could give your newbie hiker self any advice before starting the trail, what would it be?

Start slow, build your stamina, and be prepared to eat and be hungry! Take notes; write shit down. Take a ton of pictures. Every single photo I took means so much. Takes me right back to the moment. I took over 12,000 photos.

What are your top tips or advice for women wanting to thru-hike the AT?

Believe in YOU. You've got this. One step at a time.

Is there anything else you'd like to mention?

I have an exponential sense of gratitude for all things in my life: the great, the good, the bad – everything that shaped me. I am thankful. I appreciate each part of my life's journey and the time I have been blessed to spend with so many wonderful people. This gratitude has not dissipated. It's my favorite gift from my time on the trail.

20. MOO BEAR (Jennifer Cenker)

Moo Bear and I were cyber-friends long before we both started our 2017 attempt of the Appalachian Trail. We met through Facebook's Appalachian Trail: Women's Group and commiserated about our similar Morton's neuroma issues with our feet (two of hers, one of mine). Stressed out and thinking my Morton's neuroma would squash any chance I had of trying to hike the AT, I relied on Moo Bear pretty heavily for support, and she was amazing! She was always there to listen and offer advice, and best of all, she understood what I was going through.

Moo Bear's hike was different from most others in that her tramily was real family – she hiked with her teenage son!

Email: Disneybelle@cfl.rr.com

Tell me a bit about yourself.

Hi, I'm Jennifer. I am 50 years old and I live on the Space Coast of Florida. I hiked the AT with my son, and we called our hike a "flip-flop, knick-knack, paddywhack" hike in that we started out NOBO, flipped before Shenandoah National Park, summited Katahdin and then headed SOBO, did another small flip to the Whites and went NOBO again. Our first attempt was in 2017 and we were on trail for about seven months. We got back on the trail in 2018 and finished in October 2018.

How did you decide to hike the AT?

When I was in high school, I remember reading something in a book about the Appalachian Trail. I was mesmerized that there was this amazing trail that went from GA to ME. Growing up, I was in love with being outside; it was my happy place. I tried to find everything I could to read about the AT during those years and knew I wanted to hike it. My senior year in 1986, I went to my father and told him about my wish to hike the trail and asked if I could take a year between high school and college to hike it. He was not keen on the idea of me tromping alone in the woods and quickly squashed that idea. I thought about it all through college where my love of being outdoors just continued to grow and figured I could hike it when I graduated college. I was offered a teaching job soon after graduation, and at the time I thought that I should probably do the responsible thing and take the job. The dream went on the back burner again – I got married, had a son – and life happened. I had been telling my husband all about my dream to hike the AT ever since we met. We had done lots of hiking and camping as a family, and one day he turned to me and said, "It is time." We planned for almost two years before setting out.

Did you hike the AT alone? Did you have a tramily?

I hiked the AT with my teenage son who, at the time we started, was 14. My husband was not interested in long-distance hiking, and he decided to be our resupply and support from home. I missed him terribly. We would try to text as often as possible, and we would call each other when we had service. There were times that cell service was poor and we would use FaceTime to talk to each other. We carried a Garmin DeLorme so he was able to track our movements.

With our flipping around so much, it was hard to be a part of a tramily. With our first part from GA to mid-Virginia, we tended to hang with the same awesome hikers, but I was slow and so many times we would play pass and catch up. We would all wind up together at a shelter and be happy to see each other, and then they would zoom off and do big days while we would catch up with them when they would zero. Going SOBO after the Whites, we did sort of form a little family of a small knot of late flip-flop SOBOs and we all kind of stuck together. When we returned to finish the trail in 2018, we found the same scenario in that I was slower, so we would run into different sets of hikers each day. We did meet up with a number of hikers while staying at a hostel in PA. We seemed to connect with several of them and we all enjoyed hanging out together. They were much faster than us, but we stayed in touch with them fairly regularly while we all finished up our hikes. We enjoyed getting to meet new people each corner of the trail.

You hiked with your son, Deep Waters! Please tell us about the decision to do that and how it was.

When Gabe realized that I was planning an AT thru-hike, he asked if he could go with me. We introduced the AT to him in the Smokies when he was probably about four years old. We would go on family camping trips to the mountains over the years and would hike parts of the trail. He was fascinated just like me that a trail ran across the country like that. I remember one time when he was pretty young, he told me he wanted to thru-hike the trail when he turned nine, and that was when I told him that it was a dream of mine to thru-hike it. So he was only off by a few years of when he got to try a thru-hike. When we realized that this hike was really going to happen, we had some serious discussions about backup plans if he wanted to get off and I wanted to keep going, so we figured out those logistics. I wanted him to know that his decisions about things were just as important as mine and that it was his hike too. So he had a say in things like gear choices, mileage for the days, and tenting locations. As a mom, I had to put more thought into safety and making sure we were well equipped. It has been the most amazing adventure being able to do this hike together! We had our moments where we got tired of each other, and he is a teenager, so add in the rollercoaster of emotions during puberty; but I wouldn't trade it for the world. We share the camp chores and make a good team.

Did you ever feel unsafe or threatened by a person, animal, or situation?

We never felt unsafe at any time on the trail as far as people are concerned. There was one night where we had chosen to stealth camp in Virginia in this teeny tent spot in the woods. There were no other hikers anywhere and we were slow, so the main bubble had already pushed past us and we hadn't seen a single person all day. That night we heard so many animal noises right up next to the tent that the two of us were pretty much frozen. I laugh now, but at the time we were both so scared to make a noise that we were texting each other back and forth on our phones. The silly thing that we have learned is that it is usually the smaller creatures like mice, raccoons and squirrels that make the most noise at night.

Did the AT change you? If so, how?

The AT has most definitely changed me on several different levels. It has shown me that we don't need half the things that we think we do – I can be happy in a small house without all the stuff we have accumulated. It has made me more resilient and shown me that I am capable of so much more than what I thought I could do. I have learned to be more patient, and the trail has taught me to enjoy all the tiny things around us.

I spent a lot of my teenage years, for a variety of reasons, feeling like I was never good enough. Hiking the AT has given me confidence in spades and shown me that I can pretty much conquer anything. The trail taught me something I guess I never realized in that I genuinely love a challenge. The parts of the trail that I massively fell in love with tended to be the ones that everyone else complained about – sections like the roller-coaster in VA, the climb out of Palmerton, PA, and my top favorite, the Wildcats in the White Mountains, had me smiling from end to end and even made me feel giddy. The more difficult the section, the more I seemed to love it.

For my son, I think it has given him a huge confidence boost and has allowed him to see what he can accomplish if he puts his mind to something. Out of all those miles, he never once said – not once – that he wanted to quit or give up. He said that being out there and hiking the trail the way we did has sparked a love of exploring and wanting to visit new places on the planet. Hiking the trail with him showed me new sides to him that I never knew existed. He is a self-driven, strong young man.

Although I kind of lost myself in the crazy hustle-bustle of life, the trail helped me find some inner peace and, most importantly, it helped me find myself again.

Please explain the origin of your trail name.

My trail name, Moo Bear, was given to me by my son when we started hiking into Virginia. I had been dying to see a bear on the trail and we hadn't seen a single one. We were hiking into a woodsy section when I spotted a large black animal behind a tree. I gleefully started jumping up and down yelling "Bear!" and pointing like a maniac so my son could spot him. My son looked and then turned to me and asked, "Why is his tail wagging?" I was confused when a black cow walked out from behind the tree. My son thought that was the most ridiculous thing ever and proceeded to practically fall on the trail laughing. The rest of the day he would just turn to me and say "Moo," and then out of the blue, he yelled, "That's it! Your trail name is Moo Bear!"

Gabe tends to be pretty quiet around everyone else even though he is a huge goofball on the trail with me. He got his trail name, Deep Waters, at Mountain Harbor Hostel in the Roan Mountain area from the incredible Shannon. She picked up pretty quickly that he is a neat kid and said he should be called Deep Waters because, while he is quiet, he has some cool things to say, and his thoughts and soul run pretty deep.

What was the most unexpected thing that happened or that you experienced?

Several things pop out in my mind from early on our hike. The first one was after we had completed our very first trail resupply run. (Boy, was that a learning process with trying to remember what we needed, then trying to find it and then finding a shuttle to where we were staying so we could shower.) We picked a local hotel and when I was checking in, I realized I had forgotten to get wipes. We used them to bathe in the tent when there were no streams. I asked the woman if there was a gas station or anything in walking distance, and she said there was nothing. Without hesitating, she asked what we needed. I told her, and again with no hesitation, she said that she had to hit Walmart after work and would pick up a package for us. I was blown away that a complete stranger would do that for us, and sure enough, the next morning when we checked out, she had left our wipes at the desk and didn't want any money for them or for her time.

Another unexpected thing was after we hiked through the Grayson Highlands, my left knee started bothering me and did not get better. We were in Damascus, and the closest walk-in clinic on our insurance was far away in a hospital in another town. We barely managed to get a ride and were dropped off at the hospital, where we asked about the clinic. We showed everyone the address for the clinic was the same as the hospital's. But there was no clinic! We were now stuck almost 30 minutes away from the trail with no car, no cabs, no shuttle drivers and no Uber. I had no clue what to do, so I called my husband to see if he could help. A woman at the check-in desk interrupted, saying she had heard our dilemma and wanted to help. She was getting off her shift and the walk-in clinic was on her way home. I literally burst into tears in the lobby and gave her the biggest hug. On the drive over, she informed me that her daughter had thru-hiked the trail and that many strangers had reached out to help her in times of need and she wanted to pay it forward.

In 2018, when we returned to the trail after Gabe's injury, three months after I had surgery on my knee, I knew that getting back on the trail was going to be slow and rough. For the remainder of our 900 miles, *so* many people reached out to offer help or to join us while we hiked. A dear friend, who was on her own AT adventure with her sweet dog, hiked the first month with us. A gracious woman offered to help us get started back on the trail. She unbelievably let us stay in her house and drove us to the trail and back each day, and we spent many hours enjoying cooking meals and eating together. A wonderful mom and daughter came out to hike for a day with us, and they treated us to dinner in town later that night. We have made some amazing friends and memories along our AT miles.

Tell me your favorite hiker trash or funniest moment.

Gabe and I like to make up ridiculous stories and songs

together when we are hiking. He will start a story and we will toss it back and forth with each of us continuously adding to the story. Each story tends to get more ridiculous than the last one. Gabe has a longer stride than me, so he tends to be a little further out in front of me, so to do our stories he has to be louder so I can hear and vice versa. This one particular day, we had been nursing a story back and forth for literally two to three hours. It revolved around Elon Musk being in cahoots with evil penguins who were all trying to take over the planet together. It was an epic masterpiece of silliness. We came to a point in the story where, out of the blue, we heard someone dying laughing, and we both turned around to see a hiker behind us. Gabe turned bright red. The hiker said he had been behind us for at least a half an hour listening in on our story and loved every second of it – said we both had some unreal imaginations.

Favorite trail food?

Mine has to be instant potatoes with a bit of gravy powder, a small packet of Velveeta-type cheese with those crispy, fried onions you usually put on a green bean casserole for the holidays. Deep Waters' is macaroni and cheese with bacon bits and he loves stroopwafles.

I know you and Deep Waters experienced some injuries. Please tell me about them.

We both managed to get injuries on the trail.

Around 800 miles in, my knee started hurting, so I went to a clinic where I was informed I had tendonitis and needed a week or two of rest. So we holed up in a cheap motel in

Marion, VA for about nine days. The knee felt better until I took a fall in the Whites in NH. I luckily found a sports medicine specialist who found nothing significant in the MRIs – it was tendonitis and I had to take a few days to rest again. It felt better after a rest but remained slightly achy for the rest of our time on the trail in 2017.

After the 1300-mile marker, we were hiking into the Rutland, VT area when Deep Waters told me his foot was bothering him. He never complained about any issues on the trail other than when we both had bronchitis and had to take a few days recouping. His feet never bothered him and he had zero blisters, so I took it seriously that he was complaining of pain. We gave his foot a rest and then tried a short one-mile hike with no pack, but it was too painful to continue. At a clinic we got the diagnosis of a stress fracture and the news that our hike was done for the year. Back at home, an orthopedic surgeon put him into a boot and he had physical therapy.

Once Deep Waters' foot was taken care of, I met with an orthopedic surgeon who determined after several MRIs that I had torn the meniscus on my knee in two places –one vertical tear and one horizontal tear along with some other issues in that knee. So I had surgery to remove the damaged meniscus. Several months of physical therapy and strength training finally got me back in shape to finish the trail in 2018.

How was hiking the AT empowering for you as a woman?

Many of the questions that came up the most when I shared

with people that I was going to hike the AT all revolved around safety and my being a woman and how would I handle problems without having a man there to help me – drove me crazy! I have always been pretty independent, so it never dawned on me to worry about how I would handle things out there. The one thing I am very self-conscious of is that I am not a svelte person. I am a larger 5'9", 210-pound woman; I don't look like your average hiker. When Gabe was born, my thyroid went belly-up and I was diagnosed with Hashimoto's disease. I went from having a skinny, athletic build to putting on a ton of weight, and my self-confidence plummeted. Since then, I have struggled with weight and with getting correct medication doses for my thyroid. I know I was behind the eight ball when I started the trail: I would be carrying the weight of my pack and my larger body up, down, and around mountains for months. I did train for over a year to prepare for the trail, so knew that I was probably in the best shape I had been in a long time.

About 600 miles into our journey, something clicked in my head. I was in a gas station bathroom, washing my face and hands, and I looked in the mirror. When I saw my reflection, I felt confident, proud, and so darn strong as a woman. I came out of there with a lighter spring in my step.

Something that will always stick with me is a moment that happened in the White Mountains in NH. I loved every single mile of the Whites, despite the fact that they are some of the harder miles on the trail. We were scrambling up a long, steep mountain, and I was out of breath and had taken a short break. A skinny, athletic woman stopped next to us and gave me the "up and down" that I had gotten a few times while on trail. Looking at my 210-pound body, she told me in a very condescending voice that the section we were on was listed as a very strenuous trail and that maybe I should find a much easier trail to hike. I was blown away that this pretentious woman would make such a judgment about me out loud. I will never forget that moment because I stood up tall, looked her square in the face and told her that she had no right to judge my hiking ability based on my looks. I shared proudly that my son and I were thru-hiking and that we had hiked over 1,000 miles of the Appalachian Trail. She was completely taken aback and the look on her face was priceless. Needless to say, I hiked on with my head held high and feeling incredibly strong and proud.

What was hardest thing about your hike?

Hiking with a partner who happened to be my son and being a mom – having to keep Gabe in my thoughts concerning safety, health, nutrition and things like that.

It was hard enough making sure to remember those things for myself and I had to do it for two people. He is very capable of looking after himself, but he is 15 and can be an impulsive teenager, so he doesn't always think about things like making sure to eat enough calories to keep his engine running.

I knew that hiking with him was going to be different than doing it by myself. We would need to make compromises that we might not be happy about, and if we had issues, we couldn't split up and finish our hikes separately like many other hikers. Some days we didn't get along at all and found ourselves quibbling over everything. I liked getting up early to watch the sun rise, make coffee and listen to the trail come alive each morning while he liked to sleep in as long as possible and would grumble about me waking him up. He liked hiking hard and fast while I liked to take my time and would drive him nuts while I looked at every mushroom, tiny forest creature, or "blade of grass" according to him. We took a bit figuring out how to make our differences work together so that we could both enjoy the adventure. We always managed to sort it out and went back to being our crazy, silly selves together while singing ridiculous songs or acting goofy.

Were there any sacrifices you had to make prior to pursuing your thru-hike?

Absolutely! I run an artist business at home while my husband works, and we both had to start socking money away in the bank to cover the hike. I put in longer hours than normal, and my husband got creative in looking at our expenses. We discussed and then made cuts in the budget and talked to our banks and insurance agent about ways to lower other expenses. We cut out spending on frivolous purchases and things like going out to eat. Family vacations were put on hold, and all the extra money was put into a savings account for the hike. We saved for almost two years for our hike.

Did you have any fears or concerns before your hike? If so, how did you deal with them on trail, and how do you feel about them now?

The only two things I was concerned about was keeping Gabe safe and making sure we had a plan in case he didn't want to continue the hike and I did. We figured out that Dave would come and get him. Dave could work from home, so he could be home with Gabe while I continued. We also tossed around the scenario of my wanting to come off the trail and Gabe wanting to continue. Neither of us was super comfortable about the idea of a 14-15-year-old on the trail alone. We discussed things like shadowing him along the trail with my Jeep. When Gabe got injured, we had to have a hard discussion. I was devastated about possibly ending my 30-year dream of completing a thru-hike, but I knew he was definitely done with a fractured foot. We had a family pow-wow, and Gabe shared that we were the Snail Brethren and that "snails stuck together" and he would be upset if I continued on without him. So we made the heart-breaking decision to end our thru-attempt and to return to the trail after he healed. We definitely made the right decision. At home, we got him under the care of a pediatric orthopedic surgeon, and I had my knee taken care of as well. It still hurts knowing that we won't be able to call ourselves true thru-hikers because we didn't finish in one continuous 12-month period. I am incredibly proud that we jumped right back onto the trail as quickly as possible to finish what we started the year before. I am proud to call myself a 2,000-miler.

Did you have any post-trail depression? If so, how did you get through it?

I experienced post-trail depression twice in our adventure – once when we stopped for the six-month recovery period and again after we completed the remaining miles.

During our recovery, I went into a low funk. I knew I would

– I just didn't realize how low I would feel. We went from having an epic adventure every day on the trail to sitting around like couch potatoes because we had to heal. It was a jolt to our bodies and to our emotional states. I think I felt it much worse than Gabe because I was coming to terms with ending a life-long dream of being a thru-hiker. I missed the many trail friends we made along the way. I love my friends back home, but I couldn't have the same conversations with them about my passion for the outdoors and everything AT-related. I had changed: things I thought were important before no longer were. But knowing that we would be returning to the trail as soon as our doctors gave us the all-clear, we dove head-first into re-evaluating gear choices, swapping out gear and planning our remaining miles.

After completing the Appalachian Trail, I felt like I was losing a dear friend as we made the long, three-day drive home. The AT had became part of me – my soul and heart – and I feel like I left a large chunk of myself out there on the trail. Gabe said he feels the same – just maybe not as deeply as I do. As I write this, we have been home for about a week and I feel a little lost right now. But I made myself a promise: I have a long list of bucket items and dreams I want to follow, and I am no longer going to sit around like I have for the past 20 years and just fantasize about them. I plan to share my photography with others and to make a business out of my passion for capturing moments with my camera. We are discussing the John Muir Trail and the Laugavegur Trail in Iceland. I think Gabe has gotten a taste of wanderlust and loves it, so I am happy now that he will have a life-long interest in traveling and following his dreams.

Do you view life differently in any way after hiking the trail?

Yes, I have noticed several changes. The trail has given me a sense of inner peace and taught me how to prioritize things in my life now. I have found a sense of who I am and in what direction I want to take myself, thanks to the trail. I have found that I am much more able to say *no*. I was always the person who could never say no to anyone, and I would quickly be overwhelmed with an insane schedule and be spread way too thin because I didn't want to let anyone down. Many of those things I did out of obligation and not because I truly wanted to do them. Life is too short to focus on things that are not worth worrying about.

If you could give your newbie hiker self any advice before starting the trail, what would it be?

Don't overthink or overplan everything. Do your research, make your choices, and if you are happy, stick with them. I spent *so* much time planning every single aspect of our hike to the finest details. I even carried around a huge notebook with labeled sections, so I could keep notes on everything from gear to trail food. It was just silly. We threw out almost everything we planned by the end of the first week on the trail.

We were happy with 99.9% of our gear choices and glad we had researched it so thoroughly. But we would make gear decisions only to find that new gear was getting released, so we would go back and second-guess our decisions. It was like a never-ending circle of choices. We also planned food drops. We picked 12 spots on the trail that were known for being poor resupply areas, and we filled 12 pre-labeled boxes with food – *huge* waste of time and money. We found that we got pretty sick of many of our original food choices a month or so into the trail, so we were stuck with a ton of food at home that we didn't want. My poor husband had to either eat it, bring it into the office for co-workers or throw it away. It was also a pain to figure out where we were going to be in order to mail the box in time for us to pick it up. It was so much easier to wing it and figure out resupply while we were on the trail.

Don't overplan by figuring out how many miles you think you will do every day. Just go with the flow, enjoy yourself and take your time. We were feeling a bit stressed by the time we hit Virginia, and I kept thinking we weren't making enough miles, that we weren't going to make it to Katahdin before it closed for the season. We finally decided to flip, so we summited Katadhin and started heading southbound. The huge wash of relief over us was pretty unreal. Now we could putz and putter and take as much time as we wanted to enjoy every aspect of the trail.

What are your top tips or advice for women wanting to thru-hike the AT?

Don't put your dreams on the back burner for a better time because that time may never happen. I put off my AT thru-hike dream for 30 years, hoping for a better time to come. While I loved every aspect of my hike – the good, the bad, the ugly – I do wish that I had done it when I was younger and my body didn't have the lovely signs of aging.

Make sure that you come prepared mentally and physically

with the right gear needed for the right weather. When the temperatures were in the teens with snow in the Smokies, or when we had high winds in the Whites, we were thrilled to have the right gear, solid shell jackets, and layers that we trusted. We saw hikers with lightweight gear that was not doing a good job, and they were miserable.

Anything else you'd like to mention?

The Appalachian Trail is something incredibly special that just can't be put into words. While you are on this mind-blowing journey, take the time to breathe it all in. Don't focus on the miles. Focus on the journey, the adventure, the beauty, and just be there in the moment.

21: ATTICUS (Jessa Victor)

I first saw Atticus, aka Attie, on the trail a week into my hike. Sunsets and I were packing up our tent one morning as she breezed out of the campsite, calling out a cheery *good morning* with a steaming mug of coffee in her hand. She seemed so put together! She was packed up and headed out well before 7 a.m. I had given up coffee on the trail, and her coffee smelled so enticing. I soon met her and discovered she was one of the kindest hikers on the trail.

Tell me a bit about yourself.

I started the trail at 25 years old and turned 26 while on the AT. I live in Madison, WI. I hiked the AT northbound in 2017, with my start date being March 23, 2017. I finished 4 months and 25 days later on August 17, 2017.

How did you decide to hike the AT? I know you're a runner; did this have anything to do with your decision?

I've always had an adventurous spirit, but I was officially bitten by the hiking bug while studying abroad in Cape Town, a South African city nestled in the Table Mountain Range. It was there I fell in love with climbing mountains, such that when I first learned of the AT, I knew it was going on my bucket list!

Being a runner didn't necessarily nudge me to hike the AT; however, it gave me the confidence I needed to know that I could push my body beyond my preconceived limits. In turn, having hiked the AT gave me the confidence I needed to branch into ultramarathon running upon my return home. I guess my love for running feeds my love for hiking and vice versa.

Did you hike the AT alone? Did you leave family, and how did you cope with missing them? Did you have a tramily at any point?

I did hike alone in that I did not come to the AT with a hiking partner. That said, I met a few hiking partners along the way. In fact, I met Tyler (who would later be named Theory) at the Springer Mountain parking lot and hiked with him all the way to the Smokies. From there, I hiked with all different hikers, but never the same hiker for more than a week or two. Regardless, it doesn't take long to form lasting friendships on the AT!

I did leave family behind, including my new fiancé. This was a constant struggle for me as I knew they were missing me terribly, and of course, I missed them. The pull to return home was made even more difficult by the fact that my fiancé had planned an epic summer road trip for himself and our dog, which I would have been a part of but for my AT hike.

At first, my fiancé and I were talking or texting almost every day. But I began to discover that this pattern was emotionally draining as it constantly reminded me how much I missed him. Accordingly, we made a pact to only talk once per week. Of course, if either of us were having a particularly challenging day, we would call more often and the other would always pick up. This arrangement worked better because our weekly phone calls became a cherished event, and I looked forward to filling him in on all that had happened over the last week rather than spending the call lamenting how much I missed him.

Unfortunately, there was no magic recipe for coping with missing family. Though I did find that distraction helped, as did reminding myself that our separation would not be permanent.

Did you have any hiking or overnight camping experience before hiking the AT?

I had gone on a few backpacking trips prior to embarking on the AT. However, prior to the AT, my longest backpacking trip had only been two or three days. Regardless, I think that was sufficient preparation as you don't often go more than three to four days without the option for a town stop while on the AT. Additionally, before the AT, I had done quite a few long day-hikes as I spent a summer as a camp counselor in Colorado and spent each free moment I had hiking in Rocky Mountain National Park.

I know you struggled with quitting at one point. Please tell us about it and how you overcame it.

Despite my innate qualities of shyness, I thrive off human companionship. But, after a week or so on the trail, self-doubt began creeping in. As a result, I felt vulnerable and began isolating myself from other hikers. Instead of camping at shelters with other hikers, I hiked on to stealth sites to camp alone. But camping alone only made me feel more depressed. And of course, when feeling depressed, the last thing I wanted to do was socialize. This vicious cycle continued until one day it became too much to bear. I pulled out my cell phone in the middle of the trail and arranged for a shuttle to pick me up at the next road crossing. My plan was to get a ride into the nearest town, which happened to be Marion, VA, check into a hotel room for the evening, rent a car the following morning, and drive straight home that next day.

Upon arriving in town, I checked into a hotel and called my mom to inform her of my plan. Despite being supportive of my decision, she also (thankfully) challenged me to reconsider. She knew I had wanted to hike the AT for years and years. She also knew that I spent countless time, effort, energy, and financial resources planning for this trip. Therefore, her position was that I owed it to myself to take my time with the decision to quit. Her suggestion was that, instead of sitting in a hotel room alone in VA trying to make this decision which would likely have led to me deciding to quit, I should call my uncle who lived nearby and stay with him for a few days while I pondered this decision. So that's what I did.

My uncle picked me up the following day and I ended up spending a week with him and his family, which was exactly the support and socialization I needed. Moreover, other family members who happened to be living in Atlanta drove up to stay with us as well. On top of that, my mom flew down from Wisconsin to stay with us too! This outpouring of family support gave me the confidence I needed to get back to the trail. At the end of the week, I rented a car. But this time, the plan was to drive back to the AT, not home.

Once back on the trail, I made sure to have a plan in place to deal with the loneliness and anxiety. First, I promised myself that I would cease camping alone. No matter what, I always camped at a designated camping site or a shelter to ensure that I would not be alone, and therefore not subject to the intense feelings of loneliness that I experience while in the woods alone at night.

Second and most important, I narrowed my focus to only the next 12 hours (sometimes only the next 6 hours) of my day. Previously, I became overwhelmed when I thought about all the miles I had left to hike, when I was going to get to the next town and where I was going to stay, or the rough weather that was forecasted for the following week. Instead, by bringing my focus to just those few hours that lay ahead of me, I was able to let go of all those extra worries. Doing so was so liberating! I realized I couldn't control next week's weather, how many miles I had left to get to Katahdin, or whether the next town's hostels would have space for me. But I could control my movement over the trail that lay directly ahead of me. This realization was grounding and comforting.

Even in post-trail life, I use this visualization when my days get particularly busy or stressful!

Did you ever feel unsafe or threatened by a person, animal, or situation?

I was never threatened nor encountered an unsafe situation related to an animal encounter (though I still maintain that the biggest danger on the AT are ticks). Additionally, I never felt threatened by another person nor felt in an unsafe situation while on the trail. However, once while at a McDonald's during a town stop, a man approached me to chat about my thru-hike. He seemed genuinely interested and harmless at first, but soon persistently tried to convince me to go to his house with him so he could take photos of me "for a photo essay." It definitely was an uncomfortable situation at best. I declined his offer and stayed at the McDonald's (in a public place) until I knew for certain he had left.

Did the AT change you? If so, how?

The trail showed me that chasing a dream is not always fun or pretty. Instead, it can be quite ugly and graceless. There were many days on the trail that I was absolutely miserable. Yet, I carried on. And that, for me, was the most beautiful part. I learned that even in these moments of terrible sadness, loneliness, and frustration, I am capable of moving forward. This was an incredible lesson to learn, and I know I am a stronger woman for having endured it.

Please explain the origin of your trail name.

Prior to starting the AT, I was invited to join the podcast, *Mighty Blue on the Appalachian Trail*, for a season. They were looking for a 2017 thru-hiker to virtually follow via weekly podcast updates. As I was preparing for my hike, we thought it would be fun to have listeners suggest trail names for me. One listener suggested Atticus after the lawyer, Atticus Finch from *To Kill a Mockingbird*. I had just recently graduated law school and thought it was pretty fitting. And so, I became Atticus. Though my full trail name was Atticus, many fellow hikers called me "Attie" as I thought this was a more feminine and peppy version of Atticus (and therefore fit my personality).

What was the most unexpected thing that happened or that you experienced?

I did not expect that I would credit my completion of my 2017 thru-hike to other hikers. I embarked on my AT hike as a solo hiker. I interpreted this to mean that I, and I alone, would have to get myself to Maine. I thought I would have to build myself up when I was feeling down and rely on my own inner strength when the going got tough.

Unfortunately, I hit a point where I realized I just couldn't get myself to Katahdin.

Fortunately, I met other hikers (shout out to The Machine and Bananas) who made up the difference. In sum, I didn't expect to owe my Katahdin summit to two strange men I met in the woods! But their energy, enthusiasm and compassion are what got me there.

Favorite hiker trash or funny moment?

I watched someone resupply at a state park's vending machine.

Favorite trail food?

I loved making my specialty tuna wrap for lunch. It was comprised of one packet of tuna on a Trader Joe's whole wheat tortilla with half an avocado, one cheese stick, and one packet of mayo. As to the avocado, I would store the other half in my cooking pot until lunch the following day (keeping the pit in the stored half helps it stay fresher longer). As to the cheese sticks, I would be sure to purchase the individually wrapped sticks, which hold up surprisingly well on the trail; in fact, I would eat them even after six days without refrigeration. Finally, as to the mayo packets, I would always "borrow" these from fast food restaurants during a resupply trip into town.

How did you feel on the day you finished your hike?

Honestly, I was ready to be done! I certainly felt proud of what I'd accomplished, but I was mostly physically and emotionally exhausted. For that reason, I did not experience an overwhelming sense of emotion. That came later while I was shopping at Trader Joe's. I had this strange realization that just a few days ago I was standing on top of Katahdin at the end of such an amazing feat. But now I found myself right back in my normal routine, standing in the dairy aisle trying to decide between soy or coconut milk. It was an overwhelming and difficult to explain moment, and I started crying right there in the Trader Joe's dairy aisle.

How was hiking the AT empowering for you as a woman?

I'm so thankful to live in a time where the backcountry is no longer a man's world! In fact, while on the trail, my identity as a woman came second to mine as a hiker. Fellow hikers treated me simply as another hiker. We were all out there hiking the same terrain, enduring the same weather, and chasing the same goal.

What was hardest thing about your hike?

The hardest part for me was being away from my friends and family. They are a constant source of strength and confidence for me. Without them, I had to hold my head high on my own. Though this was the hardest part of my hike, it was also the most rewarding.

Were there any sacrifices you had to make prior to pursuing your thru-hike?

I sacrificed spending time with my family and friends in order to hike the AT. I missed birthdays, wedding showers, and family vacations. Thankfully, I have supportive friends and family who understood my desire to hike and were forgiving of the fact that I could not be present for them for a few months.

Did you have any fears or concerns before your hike? If so, how did you deal with them on trail, and how do you feel about them now?

I was concerned about the weather. I hate being cold and wet, and therefore spent a substantial amount of time and energy at the beginning of my hike trying to avoid and to plan my hikes around bad weather. Eventually, I finally accepted the fact that I would not be able to avoid all the rain between Georgia and Maine. Instead, I became an absolute pro at setting up and taking down my tent in the rain and always made sure I had a dry set of sleeping clothes in my pack. With this skill under my belt, I knew that, even if I got soaked on my hike, I would be dry at night. This was a comfort during some very long, cold, and wet stretches of trail.

Now when I get caught in the rain on a run or a bike ride, I am often overcome with a sense of gratitude for the fact that I have a dry and warm home to return to. I hope I never lose this feeling!

Did you have any post-trail depression? If so, how did you get through it?

Thankfully, I did not struggle with post-trail depression. Upon my return home, I threw myself into a new career, wedding planning, and ultramarathon training. Between these three new adventures, I was able to stave off the depression. That said, I am often hit by waves of nostalgia and a longingness to be back on the trail on a daily basis.

If you could give your newbie hiker self any advice before starting the trail, what would it be?

Though I am naturally shy, I thrive off companionship. I would remind myself, that although it seems so much easier and comfortable to be a tent hermit, sometimes sitting around the campfire and swapping stories with your fellow hikers will be life changing.

Also, try to meet hiker friends of all ages! Generational diversity is a beautiful aspect of the AT. Walking the whole trail with only those of your similar age is like walking the trail with only one eye open. You won't get the full picture.

What are your top tips or advice for women wanting to thru-hike the AT?

Forget politeness! Now, let me clarify – that does not mean that you should skip being kind. Instead, what I mean is this: as women, society teaches us to be accommodating, submissive, and passive, even if someone else's behavior is making us uncomfortable. Because of this, we are often more concerned about hurting others' feelings than we are of our own comfort and sometimes safety. Being polite is admirable, but don't let it compromise your safety or your experience. If someone is making you uncomfortable, say something or get away from him or her without feeling guilty about potentially hurting their feelings. You don't always have to be the polite woman society taught you to be.

Anything else you'd like to mention?

Care about your nutrition! Typically on the trail, the anything-goes mentality kicks in when it comes to food. And it's mostly true. During a thru-hike you will find your caloric needs significantly increase, perhaps to a point that it may become difficult to keep up. This leads many hikers to devouring the cheapest, highest calorie foods that are available at the Dollar General. I have no qualms with this approach except that it sometimes leads to neglect of our female bodies' unique nutrient/mineral needs. For example, I became low in iron, which led to daytime fatigue. As a result, I started to seek out foods with higher iron which helped my energy level and therefore my ability to get up and over those mountains during the day.

So in addition to the typical hiker diet, try to make sure you are fueling your body in a wholesome way. Pay attention to how you're feeling and keep in mind that what you're putting in your body may have something to do with it. By no means should you forgo the Snickers, bottomless bowls of ice cream, and entire pizzas; but try to add in some fruits, veggies, healthy fats, and complex carbs on top of that. You will likely feel better, both physically and mentally, for doing so.

22. MYSTIC (Kim DeGrazia)

At first, I only knew Mystic through the Appalachian Trail: Women's Group on Facebook, as she had bought some of my handmade hiking jewelry. Then, when I was on the trail, she came up to me at one of the shelters as I was eating my mashed potatoes and introduced herself – I'm so glad she did! We became fast friends after that, often running into each other on the trail or in camp or in hostels.

Mystic was a solo hiker who dealt with her fear of heights while on the AT. I admired her courage for being out there climbing on boulders and cliffs with drop-offs everywhere on a daily basis.

Facebook: facebook.com/kim.degrazia

Tell me a bit about yourself.

I live in the foothills of North Carolina. I hiked the AT in 2017, at age 56. Started at Springer Mountain, GA, on March 20 and headed NOBO. I made it to just past Dragon's Tooth (700 miles) before getting off due to knee injury from a fall. I was going to ignore it, but I woke up the last few mornings prior to getting off unable to walk at first, second or third try, so I decided to have it checked out. I had cracked the inside of my kneecap. I got off the trail on June 1, 2017.

How did you decide to hike the AT?

Deciding to hike the AT was actually a slow process. I was doing day hikes on the Ice Age Trail (IAT) in Wisconsin starting about 15 years ago. I did a weekend hike in Southern Kettle Moraine with my son and got the hiking bug. I was working 50- to 60-hour work weeks and hiking was a way to get back some sanity. I read a lot about the IAT and from there articles on the AT started popping up. It became a "when I retire I am going to hike the AT" mantra. We moved from WI to NC in 2012, and I started making the mantra into a reality. I hiked many local trails in the mountains to start getting in shape and attended a Rogue Dames weekend seminar on hiking in 2016. I met a woman from Utah who also wanted to hike the AT, and we started making plans for the following spring.

Did you hike the AT alone? Did you leave family, and how did you cope with missing them? Did you have a tramily at any point?

I intended to hike with J-Walk (Joyful Walkabout) and we started the trail together on March 20th. She had to get off trail when we hit Mountain Crossings as her feet were just covered in blisters (she did get back on and ended up hiking 200 miles). So it was solo from then on. I left my husband at home with the dogs, and he was placed in charge of the house and bill pay, which was a big learning curve as I always paid the bills. He also sent my food boxes every week. He did wonderfully! We kept in constant contact via cellphone. If there was an area where cell service was sketchy, I would let him know so he wouldn't worry about not hearing from me for a few days. I never had an official tramily but did meet up with the same people (Chica and Sunsets!, Sushi Roll and Roar) over and over again.

Did you have any hiking or overnight camping experience before hiking the AT?

Overnight camping consisted of a weekend with my son, and I also did an overnight with a Rogue Dame meetup at Grayson Highlands prior to the AT hike. The latter overnight was a great experience as it got down to 20 degrees with 40-mile-an-hour winds, so it was very cold. It didn't scare me.

Did you ever feel unsafe or threatened by a person, animal, or situation?

I only felt "weirded out" in one situation but never felt unsafe. This was in VA just before the Mount Rogers Recreation Area Visitor Center. I was hiking behind a man and he paused to let me pass. I asked him how he was doing, and he said that people were being very mean, mainly online on his phone, and it felt like a thousand tiny knives sticking into him. Ho-kay. I heard that the next night he was staying in the Partnership Shelter, which was right next to the visitor center, and woke everyone up at midnight screaming that someone stole his stuff. He was so erratic that the police were called. At no time did he become violent. He was just "off." This incident was passed up and down the trail so other hikers could be warned. I heard nothing after that, so hopefully he decided to stop his hike. I saw no elk, wild pig, or bear on the hike, and only two rattlesnakes. They did not scare me.

Did the AT change you? If so, how?

Yes! I am more confident in my ability to find a way to solve problems. For instance, I was getting ready to set up the hammock one evening and found that one of the tree straps was no longer in my backpack. I had to figure a way to rig it up so I could sleep that night. Also, spring rain caused rivers to rise and crossing some of them was a real challenge. There was one river where it was obvious a tree was used as the way to get over it. Unfortunately, another tree had fallen on top of it and there was no way to use it. I took off my boots, tied them around my neck, and made sure that it was only up to thigh deep where I crossed. The water flow was fast and the river washed into a much larger river not far below where I was crossing, which made it a bit scary. Another hiker was going in the opposite direction and had just crossed where I was about to go. I asked him if he wouldn't mind waiting until I got across. He waited. I made it, wobbly and barefooted. Having a person to watch made the crossing easier, and it was safer to have another person there just in case something happened. There was never the thought of not continuing; you just have to understand the problem and figure the solution while staying safe.

I also am more accepting of people who are "different" from myself. I no longer pass a scruffy, unkempt person on the street without at least saying hello. Some are surprised, but appearances don't stop me. Everyone has a story to tell and I like to hear the stories. We may all have different backgrounds and beliefs, but it's amazing the ways we are also alike.

Please talk about your fear of heights and how you coped with this on the trail. Did you overcome your fear at all?

I have a gut-wrenching fear of heights, mainly when standing in a wide, open area with no support. Most of the AT is in woods. If I fall, there will be a tree to stop me. However, there are a few places that are open and steep. This didn't happen often and that part of the trail didn't last long enough for me to become frozen with fear. I became too busy trying to place my next step, figure out whether to use the poles or just drop them down, take off the backpack or leave it on. If there were other hikers, I would try to focus on where they were walking, my sight on their feet and not on the heights. Problem solving kept the fear at bay. I can't say anything north of 700 miles, but I can say that the seat of my pants would most likely be worn down if I kept going, especially on Mt. Washington and Katahdin! Heights did not stop me from hiking.

There are a few places that offer an alternate trail. I did take one in an area just north of the Great Smoky Mountains National Park. I was hiking with my brother-in-law and his sister. The sister also has a great fear of heights. One part had a sign that stated there was a great boulder field and it was on the edge of the mountain. We took the other trail and did not feel like we were skipping part of the AT. The alternate trail was just that and was also considered part of the AT.

Please explain the origin of your trail name.

I got my trail name in the first week. J-Walk and I both had gravity filters and hers kept stopping up. I was able to fix it each time. So something with water in it was mentioned, Miss Janet (a trail angel) said "water witch," but people kept hearing "water bitch," so that was out of the question. J-Walk said it was almost magical, maybe mystical. So Mystic Waters came about and it was shortened it to Mystic.

What was the most unexpected thing that happened or that you experienced?

The most unexpected thing I experienced was loneliness and boredom. How so? Heading northbound there are always people. It can get downright crowded at the shelters in the evening. Still, there were many hours I was by myself as I am a slower hiker. I started to miss my family at home. It got into my head. Boredom, also. You wake up, eat and break camp, then walk. You stop for the night, set up camp, eat, talk. Next day it's the same thing. So you develop a routine. You need to be aware that this also can get into your head and take steps to make sure this doesn't happen. Download music, audiobooks from the library. NPR seemed to be a popular thing people listened to. Take more pictures. Stop and smell the air. Take the side trails! Understand that this is a rare opportunity and you worked hard to get it.

Favorite memory from the trail?

Just one? There were many!

• Meeting people who actually lived on the trail was eye opening. A woman named Hopper hiked the trail each year and would work at a hostel in the winter. She said it was cheaper than renting an apartment.

• Singing "The Hills are Alive" from the Sound of Music on top of a bald.

• Singing at all, only because I am so tone deaf. Maybe that's why I never saw a bear!

• The awesomeness of trail angels.

• Meeting people named Venom, Ramblin' Man, Nightcrawler, Krazy Korean, Rowdy and her dog Steve, Crayola, Malibu, Thunda. Two chefs who cooked fresh food and carried a small iron skillet.

• The people who would get water for me at camp. Water is usually straight down from the camp. A steep and long trail. I would be so tired at the end of a long day. I carried extra food as an enticement for other hikers to help me fetch water, and hiker hunger was real for many. Saved my legs for the next day's hike many times.

• Chica and Sunsets. Sushi Roll and Roar. My home will always be open for them.

• Meeting Nighthawk. She's from my hometown of Kenosha, WI, and went to school with my nephew. Graduated high school half a semester early and took off on the trail. Never met her prior to the AT! A true badass.

• The towns: Hiawassee, Franklin, Hot Springs, Damascus. Always there just when you need them.

• A spider web glistening in the morning sun.

• The spring flowers carpeting the Smokies.

• Peeing in the woods and having a deer walk up and start eating plants right next to me.

• Bear bags swinging in the breeze.

• Hanging in the hammock with a thunderstorm rolling through. Thunder, lightning, wind. My tarp held up. I saw people hanging onto their tents from the inside. Amazing.

• Sleeping in a cloud (don't recommend it!).

• Owls flying overhead at night and hooting.

• Coyotes close by, serenading.

• Icicles springing up from the ground.

Did you have any injuries?

I got off the trail at 700 miles due to a knee injury from a fall. I fell often, but this was a nice piece of flatness and I wasn't paying attention and most likely hiking too fast. Landed face down with a full pack on. Felt like a turtle.

Cracked the inside of a kneecap.

Tell us about how you prepped your trail food ahead of time and had it sent to you on trail.

I dehydrated much of my food: chicken, beans, sauces, jerky, *etc.* I looked up recipes, bought books, and started dehydrating about a month before my hike. I also bought dehydrated vegetables from Harmony House and followed freezer bag cooking. I would take one recipe and line up the ingredients, enough for 10 meals. I got a food saver bag and would go down the line, plunking everything in. I had a small baggy for spices and created a separate line for those. Added a freezer bag in with the meal and sucked out all the air with the food saver and – *voilà!* – 10 meals. I created 125 meals like this. Some were easy, soups and chilis from Harmony House. Ramen soup that I added dehydrated veggies to. Bought dried fruits and put them in food saver bags. Getting injured left me with a lot of meals that didn't get used on the AT, but I do hike a few days at a time now and still use these meals as they last forever.

How did you feel on the day you finished your hike?

The day I finished the hike I was very ambivalent. I didn't finish the whole trail due to injury, but I was actually ready to get off. I have come to accept the fact that long distance, for me, will last two to three months and it is fine. I will get back on the AT and I will finish it. It'll take me a couple years and that's okay. I do not need to start over again and will get back on at the 700-mile marker and continue from there. Anyone who gets on the trail with a long-distance goal is a badass hiker, no matter where they finish.

How was hiking the AT empowering for you as a woman?

The AT was empowering as it made me realize that I can solve problems on my own. Any problem. My husband tended to help me out at home and I let him; it was easy. Now that I am back, I have to tell him to back away and let me do whatever it is my own way. Not sure how to word this, but I will not let a person get by with saying or doing something that bothers me. I will speak up; I have found my voice.

What was hardest thing about your hike?

The hardest part of my hike was missing my family. We will be moving back to Wisconsin to be closer to them. Interestingly, hiking and developing hiking legs is not the hardest part of the hike. If you take it slow to start, you will eventually get your legs and not damage your feet. Lots of Vitamin I (ibuprofen) helps, too.

Did you have any fears or concerns before your hike? If so, how did you deal with them on trail, and how do you feel about them now?

There were many sleepless nights before the hike. Would it be too hard? Could I walk 10 miles a day to start? Would I have enough food to make it to the next mail drop? Would there be enough water? Bears! Heights! Storms, snow, ice, heat. I prepared well and read everything I could. Followed people on Trailjournals.com. Looked up questions on whiteblaze.net. *Youtube* was another favorite. Every question you have has an answer. I walked every day. Hiked the local mountain bike trails with my pack fully loaded.

As with everyone else who starts the AT, I carried way too much food and water. I eventually got used to knowing what to carry. Water took much longer to figure out than food.

Cold. One day, prior to the Smokies, it started raining. It rained most of the day and then it got colder. I made it to the next shelter and it was full. Stood there and immediately started shaking with cold. Was told to change my wet clothes but it was already too late. My hands weren't working and I couldn't think. Hopper had her sleeping bag out and got me wrapped up in it until the shaking stopped. I made some coffee and started to warm up. Didn't realize how bad it was until the next morning when I got my coffee and stove bag out. The inside of the bag had spilled coffee in it from the day before. I couldn't even hold the cup. It sleeted all evening and turned into snow overnight. Many people slept in the shelter and on the shelter floor. The wind brought the sleet in and covered all the sleeping bags. We were all wet and needed to get help. We hiked out the next morning and actually found a ride. He was a hostel owner and was dropping hikers off to the trail. We were very lucky as there wasn't a main road in the area. He was driving on an old gravel road. Help comes when you need it. That was the scariest part of the entire hike. Lesson learned. Don't stop moving. Jump around. Change wet clothes immediately.

All the other worries went away. The trail is easy as it passes many towns, many roads. You are never too far from civilization.

Did you have any post-trail depression? If so, how did you get through it?

I had some post-trail depression, but it wasn't too bad. I still walk every day. I am an hour and a half away from the trail and will go hike when the urge comes on. I had two surgeries and gained some weight during that time, but am now fit again and lost that weight quickly. Hiked the Foothills Trail in SC for four days. Swim, bike, keep active. I am retired and do not have a job to go back to. Very fortunate.

Do you view life differently in any way after hiking the trail?

Life is to live. It's short. Don't waste it.

What advice do you have for newbie hikers wanting to thru-hike?

Advice to a new hiker is to read and watch everything you can from people who have hiked. Do not go on a website for advice (I'm thinking Facebook here). There are many armchair experts that have no clue but will still tell you what to do. Go to the experts: watch them, read them. Go out and take a weekend to backpack if you haven't done it before. You may not like it. We just took my sister on a day hike to Charlie's Bunion in the Smokies. Her question was, "So this is what you did every day? With a heavy backpack?" The hike did not thrill her. Needless to say, she will not be backpacking with me any long distances!

What are your top tips or advice for women wanting to thru-hike the AT?

Women hikers, I highly recommend a P-Style. Buy it before and practice at home. I found it very handy in that I could unzip and pee without pulling my pants all the way down. Cleaned it out with leaves. Very handy. Didn't have to use a pee rag. The P-Style had its own little case and was hooked right in the front of my pack belt. Still use it even on day hikes.

Also, "mansplaining" is real. Be patient. I chose to be amused by it.

Anything else you'd like to mention?

If you are thinking of hiking, try not to put it off. Set a date. Start preparing. You won't regret it. Get Sunsets' and Chica's *Thru-Hiking the Appalachian Trail*. It does not tell their story, but gives you so many tips and ideas on everything from supplies to equipment to electronics to clothes to maps to what worked for them and what didn't. Very thorough.

Get out there!

23. CHICA (Jen Beck Seymour)

Surprise! Thought it would be fun to interview myself.

Tell me a bit about yourself.

I was 47 when I started my thru-hike of the AT in 2017 with my husband, Sunsets. We went NOBO and it took us 179 days, just a day shy of 6 months to hike 2,189.8 miles.

How did you decide to hike the AT?

We had been living in Costa Rica at the time, and our morning routine included hiking in the beautiful mountains of the Central Valley. We were both itching to do a new adventure, and since we were enjoying hiking so much, somehow the Appalachian Trail came up one day. I honestly can't remember who brought it up, but there it was – this new idea – out on the table. We couldn't stop thinking about it. The more we talked about the possibility of hiking it, the more excited we both got. I was surprised at myself with how excited I was! After some training and the assurance that my body could actually hike 15 miles at one time without falling apart, we decided to go for it.

Did you have a tramily at any point?

We did have what we call a "quasi-tramily" – we would see certain hikers either during the day or at camp at night, but didn't necessarily hike with them all day (although a few times we did). And we weren't with the same people throughout the whole hike. The person we were with the most was Easy Goin'; his pace was similar to ours and we just got along well with him (he was really easy-going). Our tramily included him, Mystic, Sushi Roll, Roar, Papa John, Zero Hero, Single T and Subway.

Did you have any hiking or overnight camping experience before hiking the AT?

Very little! We had done a single two-night gear test a few months before the start of our hike. We got to test all our gear, make sure everything worked, and see if we wanted to change anything; it even rained on us and we got to use our rain gear. I really had very little experience before I set out on the AT. The longest hike I had done was 15 miles.

Did you ever feel unsafe or threatened by a person, animal, or situation?

No, never. Even though we didn't always hike together, I definitely enjoyed being on this journey with my husband

and best friend. There were just a couple of times I got a creepy vibe from someone (I talk about this in Chapter 2), but other than that I felt totally safe.

As far as animals go, I only saw four bears and only fleetingly. They were all juvenile size and ran the other direction as soon as they saw us. Now we did see a lot of snakes, 37 in total, but I think part of this is due to the fact that Sunsets is a snake fanatic. He loves snakes and always seemed to find them when I walked right by (or over!) them. Oddly, we didn't see a copperhead (which was fine with me). We also got to see a moose twice in Maine, which was awesome, and we were far enough away that I felt safe.

What was the most unexpected thing that happened or that you experienced?

Making so many friends. I'm introverted by nature, and I also knew that most thru-hikers are not my age (most are younger, and the rest are older). First surprise is that I actually met several hikers my age. Second surprise is that age doesn't matter; I became friends with hikers younger and older than me.

Any favorite moments?

• Waking up groggy one morning, having a hard time getting going, and then I opened the tent flap and saw a gorgeous sunrise. Made me pause and take it all in.

• One day we had trail magic so many times, we didn't even partake in the last one to save it for other hikers.

• Hiking up a hard incline and tripping and cursing the whole way, and then getting to the top with a gorgeous view. Worth it!

• One day we got the best lunch spot – we sat on huge boulders that overlooked the valley below.

• Taking a break on trail one day, and all of a sudden Attie appeared. We hadn't seen her for a month or so and had heard she might be quitting. I later ran into her again in town and sat in the Dairy Queen talking with her for a while – it was great to see her again and know that she was still on the trail.

• One particular night camping with three others (Single-T, Sushi Roll and Roar), having rain all night, then waking up to a beautiful day and choosing to hang out and talk around the fire pit and getting a late start to hiking. Roar even made me a cup of coffee!

• Hiking one day when I was just in a bad mood. Got to a gap where a guy was grilling hamburgers and had cold sodas. It was amazing, and it turned my whole day around.

• Soaking my aching feet in a cold creek at the end of one particularly brutal day of hiking.

• Worrying about what to do with our tent after a tree branch had fallen on us during a storm. No one in town had what we needed and we didn't want to wait days to have something sent to us. Family Man, a hiker we had not met before, who was at the same hostel we were, heard our story and casually said, "Hey, I have a tent-sleeve you can have." That was all we needed, and he graciously gave his up for us! It was a little thing to him, but a *huge* thing to us.

• Hiking with friends Caryn and Keith in North Carolina for a day and a night and taking lots of breaks. They brought us all sorts of goodies – cooked us dinner, served us wine(!), made a fire and made us coffee the next morning.

• Eating as much as I wanted to without worrying about gaining weight. In fact, I lost 38 pounds while on the trail!

• Slack-packing for eight days straight in Maine with Papa John.

• Lying on my husband's chest in our tent as darkness descended and hiker chatter around us quieted down to a whisper.

• Having a really hard hiking day, choosing to change up our plans and head into Rutland, VT. Surprised to find out one of our favorite bands, Sister Hazel, was playing that night (free) at a street festival, and we even got to meet them!

• Trail angels! These people act out of the goodness of their hearts, and continuously floored me with their generosity and happy spirit. There were so many trail angels.

• One night in our tent, I was talking to Sunsets about the cooling rag and how great it was. I got it out and started whipping it around in the tent, and we got the giggles and laughed and laughed. It was a good night.

• Slack-packing one day with Easy' Goin, Tarzan, Newt and Compass, and then having drinks afterwards at a gorgeous colonial hotel (where they subtly suggested we sit outside on the deck). It was the perfect ending to a perfect day.

How did you feel on the day you finished your hike?

On top of the world! Totally badass! Both Sunsets and I felt like we had wings and flew up Katahdin. Realistically, Katahdin is a hard mountain to climb; it goes up over 4,000 feet in elevation in just 5 miles. And then you have to come back down. We were soaring high on adrenaline that day, the last day of our 179-day trek, the ending point, actually being at the famous Katahdin sign I'd been literally *dreaming* about for months. It was super-emotional summiting Big K. I tear up thinking about it even now.

How was hiking the AT empowering for you as a woman?

I liked my body before the AT, but during my trek, I came to love my body. I was amazed that my legs could carry me 20 miles a day, over roots, rocks, boulders, mountains, mud bogs, and rivers.

Being challenged every day with different terrain was hard, but after I accomplished each day, I was immensely proud of myself that I did it!

I felt empowered that I learned to like myself without doing my hair every day, without putting on makeup every day, without shaving every day. I always felt beautiful on the trail – with my naked face and buff headband – which I wasn't expecting.

I felt empowered that I could hang with the guys. I thought it was cool I had female and male friends of all ages on the trail.

What was hardest thing about your hike?

I loved almost everything about my hike, but there were also several difficulties. I guess the hardest thing was the daily challenge. You never know what each day will bring as far as terrain or mountains to climb. Sometimes I would feel like I couldn't go on: it was just too hard or steep or wet or cold. Sometimes I'd cry. Sometimes I felt like I was not having any fun. But at the end of the most difficult days – climbing a particularly hard mountain, managing to meet my goal even after a hard rain – I would feel so proud! The lowest days sometimes produced the greatest highs!

For me, this is where hiking with my partner really helped. Sunsets is not just my husband: he's my best friend. When I was having a hard day, he would be there for me. And vice versa, when he was having a bad day, I would pump him up. Luckily, it never happened that we were both having a bad day on the same day, but I think this is something that comes naturally for us as a couple in knowing how to take care of each other and knowing when to step back and be less selfish if the other needs you more.

I was worried that Sunsets would want to hike faster and ahead of me everyday, but this never happened. He said he liked hiking with me better than going fast and not being with me. However, we did have different paces on hills and mountains. Sunsets thrived on the ascents, so I would let him go ahead of me. I thrived on the descents, and he would let me go ahead of him so he could take his time and not fall coming down. We worked well together in this way, so we could both take our time when we needed to and not feel pressured. We'd always meet up later at some point.

Were there any sacrifices you had to make prior to pursuing your thru-hike?

Not really. We had already quit our corporate jobs and sold almost all of our possessions years before our AT trek when we moved to Costa Rica (best decision!). My mom was gracious enough to let us stay with her before we started the AT, which gave us a chance to gather the rest of our gear, sort everything out, and focus on our hike. We don't have kids, and we didn't have pets at the time. We also didn't have a car or a house, so the only monthly bill we had was our cell phones.

Did you have any fears or concerns before your hike? If so, how did you deal with them on trail, and how do you feel about them now?

I was concerned about bears. I even had bought some bear spray online before I started the trail. But when it was delivered, it was HUGE (always look at the measurements first!) and very heavy, so no way was I bringing that. Then I got a mini air-horn. I did bring that with me but eventually put it in a hiker box as I never used it (and there was no way I could get to it fast enough if a bear surprised me, anyway).

I was nervous about fording rivers, which we didn't encounter until we got to Maine. As it turned out, the water level never came past my thighs on any of them, and I didn't even fall in the water (my main concern).

Did you have any post-trail depression? If so, how did you get through it?

None. I think because I knew about post-trail depression, I was determined for it not to happen. What did I do to combat it? I had goals and plans lined up that I was excited about doing after my thru-hike. Sunsets and I would talk about our tip book we wanted to write and also started planning our Camino de Santiago hike in Spain. This was a future semi-long distance hike to look forward to, totally different than the AT.

Do you view life differently in any way after hiking the trail?

I am much more open to people in general. It doesn't matter what they look like (some of us hikers started looking pretty gnarly during our thru-hike). Everyone has a story.

I feel more confident about sticking up for myself and standing my ground.

I also don't feel the need to shower every single day now. Unless I work out or get sweaty, I'm just not that dirty, so why shower?

I appreciate a warm and comfy bed, hot water, ice cubes, even just a chair to sit in.

I had self-confidence before the trail, but after the trail my badassery level definitely took a spike. I still can hardly believe that I thru-hiked the whole Appalachian Trail and lived in the woods for six months. It still seems like a really good dream. I'm not sure if this feeling will ever leave me, and I'm OK with that.

If you could give your newbie hiker self any advice before starting the trail, what would it be?

Don't be so nervous! Everyone is in the same place in the beginning – no one knows exactly how to use bear cables or hang a bear bag, how to set up a tent or a tarp, how to gather and filter water, how to plan the next resupply, *etc.*

Don't worry so much about getting to Katahdin. Take one state at a time, one day at a time, one step at a time.

Don't compare yourself to other hikers in regards to speed or distance hiked each day. You don't have to be the fastest hiker out there. This was a real struggle for me, as I hiked pretty slow and there were always other hikers passing me. It didn't mean I wasn't a good hiker, but I had to constantly tell myself this.

Take more pictures of people!

What are your top tips your for women wanting to thru-hike the AT?

• Do your research.

• Plan and budget your time and money.

• Don't be too nervous about everything. The trail will provide.

• Start with low mileage and build up slowly – this will help to prevent injuries and save your sanity in the beginning.

• Take one day at a time: if you think about doing this for six months it will overwhelm you.

• **Get out there and do it!** If you never try, you'll never know all you are capable of.

V. THANK YOU

"Don't ever accept anyone else's preconceived limitations. If there's something you want to do, there isn't any reason you can't do it."

– AMY DODSON

THANK YOU for reading my book!

If you liked this book, please consider leaving a review on Amazon.com. Reviews are the easiest way to say THANK YOU to an author and to support them. Even the shortest reviews ("I liked it") count.

For more in-depth information on how to succeed on the AT, check out: *Thru-Hiking the Appalachian Trail – 100 Tips, Tricks, Traps, and Facts* (available on Amazon, Barnes & Noble and iTunes).

Please follow Sunsets and me on these social media sites as we continue to explore the AT, other trails, and adventures of all kinds:

YouTube.com/ChicaandSunsets
Facebook.com/ChicaandSunsets
Instagram.com/ChicaandSunsets
AppalachianTrailTales.com

VI: BONUS SECTION

"Be fearless in the pursuit of what sets your soul on fire."

— JENNIFER LEE

If you know me at all, you know I love a good bonus at the end of a book (all the books I've written have this). An extra little tidbit (or in this case, three!) of information that is hopefully helpful to my readers. Enjoy!

BONUS 1 – Recommendations

There are tons of books, videos and social media out there; these are just a handful of my personal favorites.

<u>BOOKS</u>

Thru-Hiking the Appalachian Trail: 100 Tips, Tricks, Traps, and Facts by Jen Beck Seymour and Greg Seymour

Appalachian Trials: The Psychological and Emotional Guide to Successfully Thru-Hiking the Appalachian Trail by Zach Davis

Take A Thru-Hike: Dixie's How-To Guide for Hiking the Appalachian Trail by Jessica "DIXIE" Mills

Grandma Gatewood's Walk: The Inspiring Story of the Woman Who Saved the

Appalachian Trail by Ben Montgomery

AWOL on the Appalachian Trail by David Miller

Push On: My Walk to Recovery On the Appalachian Trail by Niki Rellon

North: Finding My Way While Running the Appalachian Trail by Scott Jurek

In Beauty May She Walk: Hiking the Appalachian Trail at 60 by Leslie Mass

<u>YOUTUBE</u>

Chica and Sunsets (aka Appalachian Trail Tales)

Liz Kidder (Handstand)

Darwin onthetrail

Evan's Backpacking Videos

Homemade Wanderlust

Early_Riser_71

Jay's on the Trail

Crystal Weaver

<u>FACEBOOK</u>

Appalachian Trail: Women's Group

NOTE: This group is supportive, women-only, and drama free (if anything happens, the administrators shut it down quickly), and you will get a wide variety of answers and advice to all your questions.

Also, connect with your trail class on Facebook (the other people who plan to hike it in the same year) by searching: Appalachian Trail [year] Class.

TRAIL JOURNALS

http://www.trailjournals.com

Trailjournals.com is great for following other hikers currently on trails (not just the AT). It has a vast number of journals going back to the 1990s and is great for gathering information or reading others' stories. You have to create an account, but it's free. And if you don't have your own blog or website, you can use this one to share your own travel tales!

JEN BECK SEYMOUR

BONUS 2 – Chica's AT Gear List

Here is my Appalachian Trail post-hike gear list. Items in **bold** were carried by husband.

<u>THE BIG THREE (shelter, sleeping bag, backpack)</u>

• Backpack – Osprey Aura AG 50

• Trash compactor bag (to line inside of pack and waterproof the contents)

• Sea to Summit pack cover

• Sleeping quilt – Enlightened Equipment Revelation (10˚F, regular width, extra-long length)

• Sleeping bag liner – Sea to Summit Reactor Thermolite Reactor (adds 15°F warmth or can be used separately in the summer)

• Air mattress – Therm-a-Rest NeoAir XLite (women's regular)

• Pillow – Big Sky DreamSleeper UltraLight

• Window insulation kit (plastic sheet we used underneath our air mattresses – extra rain protection and helped insulate noise of air mattresses)

• Sit pad – Therm-a-Rest Z Seat

• Tyvec – tent ground cover

• **Tent – Big Agnes Copper Spur UL3**

CLOTHES/RAIN GEAR

• Puffy jacket – Mountain Hardwear Ghost Whisperer (down fill 800)

• Fleece Cuddl Duds Half-Zip Hoodie

• T-shirt – Icebreaker (women's)

• Running compression shorts – Athleta

• Leggings – Athleta

• Sports bra – Smartwool

• Underwear, 1 pair – ExOfficio Give-N-Go Sport Mesh Hipkini

• Liner socks, 2 pairs – Injinji Toesock Liners

• Hiking socks, 2 pairs – Darn Tough Light Hiker Micro Crew

• Hiking shoes (trail runners) – Salomon Women's X-Mission 3 W

• Camp shoes – Xero Z-Trails

• My favorite buff – Buff brand

• 2nd buff (kept outside of backpack) – Devil's Backbone Brewing Company

• Sleep socks, wool – REI

• Watch – Timex Ironman Triathlon

- Gloves – Zpacks Possomdown gloves

- Women's cycling sleeves

- Gaiters – UltraGam on Etsy

- Beanie hat – Choucas Hat

- Mosquito net – Walmart

- Sun hat – ExOfficio BugsAway

- Umbrella – Euroschirm (also found at Amazon and Zpacks)

- Trekking poles – LEKI Corklite SpeedLock

- Rain jacket – Patagonia

- Town clothes – Athleta skort

- Town clothes – Icebreaker women's t-shirt

EATING/WATER

- Spork – Sea to Summit Long Handle Titanium

- Shamwow

- Water bladder – Evernew Water Carry 2L

- Water filter and water scoop (half of Sawyer plastic bag) – Sawyer Squeeze

- Dry bag for food – Zpacks

- NOTE: We sent our cook stove MSR Pocket Rocket and

cooking pots home about halfway through our hike. We found that we were both too tired at the end of hiking all day to get out all the supplies, boil the water, wait for the rice to cook, and then clean up afterwards. Plus it was summer and the last thing we wanted to do was eat a hot meal. We found ourselves snacking at night more than cooking. We also knew we could hang the bear bag quicker and then be done with our duties sooner for the night. After we sent it home, we didn't miss it at all, and our packs were so much lighter!

ELECTRONICS

• Cell phone, charger, headphones – iPhone 7 Plus (256GB)

• Headlamp – Black Diamond ReVolt

• Charger – Anker PowerCore 20100

• 4-Port USB port wall charger

• Ultrapod tree wrap and tripod

OTHER

• Reading glasses (wrapped in small cloth with rubberband)

• Bandana (pee rag)

• Cooling chill rag/towel

• RunninGluv (snot and sweat rag with a loop, hooked onto my front backpack strap)

• Pocket knife (Swiss Army)

• Small brush, toothbrush, toothpaste

• Ear plugs

• TP kit (toilet paper, wet wipes, hand sanitizer, tampons)

• First aid (Bandaids, vitamin I [ibuprofen], Neosporin, Leukotape, Benadryl, KT-tape)

• Toiletries (Vaseline, nail clippers, Carmex, small mirror, tweezers, razor)

• Miscellaneous: sleep pad repair kit, bunion sleeve, Morton's neuroma pad

• Daypack – Sea to Summit Ultra-Sil

• OFF Deep Woods insect repellent

• Water bottle holder on shoulder strap of backpack. Handmade by Justin Anderson (see his Etsy shop "Justins UL").

• Zpacks wallet zip pouch

• Zpacks phone holder (backpack shoulder pouch)

• Zpacks pillow dry bag (for clothes)

• **Guidebook – *The A.T. Guide Northbound 2017* by David "Awol" Miller, and a small notebook and pen**

• **Zpacks food bag (Sunsets carried the full bear bag hanging kit, and I had a separate food bag)**

• **Pooper scooper (a 9" aluminum snow tent stake, which we wrapped extra paracord around the handle)**

See video of my AT post-hike gear here:
https://youtu.be/FM6ybnBbM_0

BONUS 3 – "How the AT Wrecked My Life"

I'd like to leave you with a little something Stacia wrote for our blog about how the Appalachian Trail "destroyed" her life. At age 26 and again at 27, Stacia attempted a solo thru-hike of the Appalachian Trail and has been addicted to long-distance hiking and the adventure lifestyle ever since. Her story struck a chord with me, how hiking can empower and alter your outlook on life.
~ Chica

Three years ago, I set out on the biggest adventure of my life. I'd never been camping before, and I'd hardly ever been hiking, but I had decided I was going to thru-hike the Appalachian Trail. I'd be lying if I told you that I had any idea the profound impact this decision would have on my life. I guess you never *really* know what all of the nuanced consequences will be of any major decision, but I'll tell you this: **The Appalachian Trail ruined my life, and it was the best thing that ever happened to me. It destroyed me.**

The Appalachian Trail ruined my ability to make small talk. I'm guilty of completely tuning out whenever the people around me are discussing who lost the football game last night or that girl from work's new boyfriend. I just have no interest in the mundane goings on that most people choose to fill their time thinking about. When you've stood on a mountain top with views for miles or camped underneath a star-filled sky, something inside of you changes. You realize that there are so many vast and important things going on in the universe. These are the things I want to talk about, not celebrity gossip.

The Appalachian Trail ruined my perceptions of humanity. Before I set out to hike a long trail, I'll admit to being wary of strangers, being skeptical of someone's intentions when they offered goodwill. I was a self-described cynic. But, after having complete strangers pay for my breakfast, bring me a cold soda "just because," leave jugs of water at a road crossing without ever seeing the face of whom they were helping, offer me a place to stay inside their home, and go out of their way to drive me somewhere I needed to be, I lost that cynicism. Now, I'm guilty of seeing the good in everyone. I have the ability to assume positive intentions even in situations that turn out badly, and my favorite person to meet is usually a stranger.

The Appalachian Trail ruined my white picket fence dream. Before the trail, I was living in a fully furnished, decorated home – with a mortgage to boot. Like a lot of Americans, I was neck deep in the rat race, placing inflated value on material possessions that I thought would make me happy. Home was a 1600-square-foot house with a huge backyard. Now, I don't make purchases if the item isn't a necessity, and I live in a 16-foot travel trailer. Rather than stability and security, I crave adventure and mobility. I don't need things. I *need* experiences.

The Appalachian Trail ruined my negative body image. I've always been chubby, and ever since I was of the age where I started comparing my body to other girls, I've been self-conscious about my weight. I won't say that the Appalachian Trail completely destroyed this feeling, but when you are literally climbing mountains day in and day out, your thoughts about your body are bound to change. For three months, my body was able to carry me and all of my earthly belongings over countless mountains for 8-10 hours a day. The longest I'd ever walked in a day prior to this was probably five miles. Three weeks into my first thru-hike attempt, I knocked out my first 20-mile day. TWENTY MILES. You could never have told me this body was capable of that. While I still struggle at times with accepting my weight, I have a much healthier relationship with my body post-hike. I'm proud of what it is capable of, and thankful that it is fit and healthy enough to continue to do everything I ask of it.

The Appalachian Trail ruined my perceptions of beauty. Before the trail, I remember being that judgy girl who wore fake eyelashes to class and thought girls didn't look "put together" without makeup. While hiking, I had somehow made it to Pearisburg, VA before I caught a glimpse of my wild and feral makeup-free face in a streaky mirror at a cheap hotel. I startled and looked away, disconcerted because I thought the girl in the mirror was beautiful, but there was no way that was *me*. I went from someone so insecure that I didn't leave the house without a full face of makeup to someone who barely wears any because I think a natural face is prettier and a dirty, sweaty, flushed face on top of a mountain is the most beautiful thing I've ever seen.

The Appalachian Trail ruined my plans for the future. Before hiking, I thought I'd get married, have a kid or two maybe, and spend my days working to pay off that house I'd bought. I had gone to graduate school and was going to become a teacher. I had a long-term boyfriend that I was planning to marry. I spent 26 years chasing this dream only to find out that it wasn't really mine. It took walking through the woods for three months to figure that out. I sold the house, I broke up with the boy, and I worked service-industry jobs for a while until I figured out what it was that I *really* wanted.

I feel like my life started the day I stepped foot on the Appalachian Trail, passed that first white blaze, and pointed my heart toward Maine. Until that moment, I'd been going through the motions that I thought I was supposed to go through. I'd been waiting for life to happen, not realizing that it was happening all around me and I was missing the point. Now, I feel as though I have crammed more life into these past three years than I experienced in all of the first 26. I've attempted two thru-hikes, each lasting two to three months. I've walked over 2,000 miles on the Appalachian Trail and countless hundreds on other trails. I've gone hiking, camping and backpacking completely alone. I moved into a camper and traveled the East Coast for a year with just my dogs for company. I've checked items off my bucket list, such as climbing a 14Ker (14,000 ft. mountain) and learning how to back a trailer. I am so much more self-assured, confident, and bold than I ever was before. I have friends all over the country that feel like family.

I'm on a course so different from the one I was on pre-hike that I often don't recognize things I said or did back then as being my own memories. I may be less financially stable… I may not be certain what the future holds… I may feel at times like I'm just blowing aimlessly in the wind… but I'm endlessly, deliriously, insanely *happy*.

**The Appalachian Trail ruined my life,
and it was the *best* thing that ever happened to me.**

Blog: https://adventurelikeagirl.wordpress.com
Instagram: https://www.instagram.com/adventurelikeagirl

VII. APPENDIX – Hiker Slang

This is taken directly from our book *Thru-Hiking the Appalachian Trail – 100 Tips, Tricks, Traps, and Facts*, which is a more comprehensive guide to thru-hiking the AT. The thru-hiking community is unique in several ways, one being that they have their own lingo. Here's our version of the most-heard slang words on the trail and their meanings.

2,000-miler: A term used by the ATC to signify a thru-hiker – even though the complete distance, which changes every year, is longer than 2,000 miles.

ATC: The Appalachian Trail Conservancy, a nonprofit organization dedicated to the conservation of the Appalachian Trail.

AT Guide (**Awol's** *Guide*): The most-used guidebook on the Appalachian Trail, available in digital and print versions (northbound or southbound, bound book or loose-leaf), by David "Awol" Miller.

Bear bag: Bag used for food and anything that smells, which is hung every night out of reach of bears and other animals.

Blazes: There are several different blazes along the Appalachian Trail, both physical (blazes) and metaphorical (blazing).

--White blaze: A 2" x 6" vertical rectangle painted on trees, rocks or signposts showing the way on the Appalachian

Trail.

--*Double white blaze:* Two white blazes, one above the other, signify an intersection or turn coming up. Two offset white blazes indicate a turn coming up, turning in the direction of the top blaze.

--*Blue blaze:* A 2" x 6" vertical rectangle on trees, signifying trails leading off the Appalachian Trail going to shelters, water sources, views or bad-weather routes.

--*Yellow blazing:* Bypassing parts of the Appalachian Trail by road (named for the middle yellow line of the road).

--*Aqua blazing:* Bypassing parts of the Appalachian Trail by canoe, boat or kayak, typically through the Shenandoah National Park section of the AT.

--*Deli blazing:* One who tries to hit all of the delis (especially in NJ and NY) along the Appalachian Trail.

--*Green blazing:* One who smokes (marijuana) their way up the trail having frequent "safety meetings" with fellow green blazers.

--*Pink blazing:* A male thru-hiker trying to catch up with a female thru-hiker by clues left in the shelter trail logs/journals.

--*Banana blazing:* A female thru-hiker trying to catch up with a male thru-hiker by clues left in the shelter trail logs/journals.

--*Silk blazing:* Being the first hiker on the trail in the early morning usually means you are clearing all the silk (spider webs) from the trail.

Blow-down: Tree or limb that has fallen across the trail.

Bounce box: A box you use and keep sending ahead from post office to post office (*i.e.,* might contain a large bottle of painkillers, *etc.,* that you only want to carry a small of amount of on the trail. You take a handful for your next days out in the woods and send the large, heavy bottle forward).

Bubble: A large number of hikers hiking together for a period of time, usually starting and ending at the same campsites each night or slightly staggered.

Buff: A soft material, similar to a bandana, but sewn together so it is tubular. Can be worn in a multitude of ways on the head, around the neck, or around the wrist. Protects from sun, absorbs sweat, and covers ears in cold weather.

Cowboy camping: Camping without a shelter over you, so you are exposed to the night sky.

Day hiker: Person who is hiking for just the day.

Embrace the suck: You will hear this almost daily. It means that some days absolutely suck – with rain, heat, body aches, *etc.* – so you need to embrace these things to get through the day.

Flip-flop: A hike that begins in one direction, then at some point changes direction (*e.g.,* hiker starts in the middle at Harpers Ferry, WV, and goes north to Katahdin, ME, then flips back to Harpers Ferry and goes south to Springer Mountain, GA). Even if someone starts out NOBO or

SOBO, they can always flip. An example of a common strategy is for the NOBO hiker to flip up to Katahdin in the summer. This provides for cooler weather when naturally they would be going through New Jersey and New York, two states that can be extremely hot and humid.

Gap: A low spot along the trail, usually going through a parking lot or crossing a road.

Guthooks: The most-used app for cellphones for the entire Appalachian Trail. Runs on GPS and does not need cell data (we used it while our phones were in airplane mode).

Harpers Ferry: The psychological and traditional halfway point in West Virginia, where the Appalachian Trail Conservancy is located (not the actual halfway point, as this changes every year, but close to it).

Hiker box: A box or container at hostels, hotels, and places in town where hikers can donate unwanted items (food, clothing, gear) and other hikers can take from it freely.

Hiker midnight: Typically around 9 p.m., an etiquette observed by being quiet and dimming the lights.

Hiker trash: An affectionate term used to describe long-distance hikers who become so accustomed to the simple life on the trail that they exhibit the sometimes socially unacceptable habits associated with it (*e.g.*, doing laundry by hand in the hotel bathtub, not showering for days and smelling like it, growing a full and untrimmed beard, finding unwrapped candy on the trail and eating it because they are too hungry to care about where it came from).

Hiker hunger: Refers to the more-than-usual hunger of hikers, generally lasting for most of a thru-hike since hikers burn so many calories each day.

Hostel: An establishment along the trail that has bunks, showers, laundry, resupply and mail-drop options for hikers. A hostel will sometimes have private rooms available as well.

Hut: In the White Mountains of New Hampshire, there are huts where any hiker can make reservations to stay (usually pricey for thru-hikers). Price includes dinner and breakfast. Thru-hikers can often "work for stay" at the huts (though that means sleeping on the floor of the dining hall with people walking by all night to visit the restroom).

HYOH: "Hike Your Own Hike," a term said to fellow thru-hikers often, meaning hike the AT the way you want to, and don't necessarily do what everyone else does.

Key Swap: A way of thru-hiking the Appalachian Trail that involves two people and a car. Example: Each day, Hiker 1 starts out on the day's trail section from the south. Hiker 2 then drives to the north end of the section, parks the car at the trailhead, and starts walking south. When they meet in the middle, Hiker 2 hands the car keys to Hiker 1. When Hiker 1 gets to the car at the north end of the section, he drives to the south end of the section to pick up Hiker 2. Reasons for this: both hikers can carry day packs, they have a car to use in the evenings for going into town or to run errands, and most likely they will be able to sleep in the back of the car/truck.

Note: We met a thru-hiker who did his own type of key swap with two vehicles and just himself. He had a motorcycle and a truck – see if you can figure it out.

LASH: "Long-Ass Section Hiker," a section hiker who does long sections of the trail at a time.

LNT: "Leave No Trace," a list of principles that ask hikers to pass through the trail as though you weren't even there (don't leave any garbage, pick up after yourself, don't harm nature).

Mail drop: A method of organized resupply while hiking. This typically requires someone from home mailing packages to you according to your schedule, so you don't have to shop for groceries.

Mouse hanger: Usually seen in shelters, a cord hanging from the ceiling through a tin can with a small stick tied to the end for hikers to hang their backpacks so mice cannot get to them.

Mt. Katahdin: The northern terminus of the Appalachian Trail, located in Maine.

Nero: Short for "nearly zero" – you hike a small number of miles that day, but take the rest of the day off.

Night hiking: Hiking at night with a headlamp.

NOBO: Northbound or north-bounder, a hiker traveling north from Springer Mountain, GA, to Mt. Katahdin, ME.

Pee rag: What some women use to dry off after urinating in the woods, usually in the form of a cotton bandana hung from the back of the pack. The sunshine dries and bleaches the bandana leaving it with no scent, and it can be thrown in the wash.

Privy: An outhouse in the woods for human waste. These will vary from bearable to "you're better off going in the woods."

PUDS: "Pointless Ups and Downs," meaning the trail will go up in elevation, then down, then up again, then down again – and repeat over and over. Hikers often feel frustrated at working so hard to go up, then to come down, and then have to go up again.

Purist: A hiker who wants to pass every single white blaze.

Resupply: To obtain more food for the next section of the trail you'll be hiking.

Ridge runner: Most likely found in high-use areas of the trail, an employee of the ATC or trail-maintaining club who educates hikers and enforces regulations. Also performs trail and shelter maintenance.

Section hiker: One who hikes the Appalachian Trail in sections (taking more than 12 months to complete the whole trail).

Shelter: 1. Your own personal place you sleep in each night (could be a tent or a hammock). 2. On the trail, a three-sided structure built with a roof, the fourth side being open to the elements, usually near a water source and a privy; sometimes called a "lean-to."

Shuttle: A ride to town or to a trail head (sometimes for a fee, sometimes included with a hostel stay).

Slack-packing: Simply put, hiking with only those things you need for the day, allowing you to carry a much smaller backpack. This can be accomplished multiple ways: someone drops you off in the morning on the trail and picks you up at night; someone drops you off in the morning and you end your hike that day at their hostel; someone drops you at trail head in the morning and meets you at end of day with your pack. The point is you have help, so you only need to carry a small daypack with water and snacks instead of a fully-weighted backpack.

SOBO: Southbound or south-bounder, a hiker traveling south from Mt. Katahdin, ME, to Springer Mountain, GA.

Springer Mountain: The southern terminus of the Appalachian Trail, located in Georgia.

Stealth camping: A campsite that has been camped at before (flat areas of land for tents, usually containing a fire pit and logs) but is not in the guidebook. Also, sometimes used as a term for camping illegally.

Stile: Steps that take hikers over a fence, but livestock cannot use.

Switchback: A zig-zag trail pattern of going up a mountain, instead of going straight up - usually made to prevent erosion but is helpful for hikers as well.

Tarp: A simple piece of tent-like fabric with no door or floor.

Tent platform: A raised platform built of wood for tents to prevent erosion in that area of the woods.

Thru-hike(r): A hike or hiker of the entire Appalachian Trail within one 12-month period.

Trail angel: Someone who provides unexpected help, food, or shelter to a hiker at no cost.

Trail log or register: A notebook usually found in shelters where thru-hikers can write their thoughts or messages to other hikers. And this is where clues are found for pink or banana blazing.

Trail magic: Unexpected food or help at no cost (most welcome by thru-hikers!).

Trail name: A nickname used by a hiker. Most all section and thru-hikers have trail names. Hikers always refer to each other by trail names.

Trail town: Towns easily accessible from the Appalachian Trail, either right off the trail or a short walk or hitchhike away.

Treeline: High point of a mountain where trees stop growing due to the high elevation and climate.

Turn stile: Similar to a stile, but a zig-zag patterned structure usually with a gate that hikers can go through but livestock cannot.

Ultralight: A style of hiking that focuses on the lightest gear possible.

Vitamin I: Ibuprofen.

Widow-maker: A tree or limb that is dead but is still hanging above and could fall at any moment on your tent in the middle of the night. If it fell on a married person's tent, it could literally make someone a widow.

Work for stay: Working for lodging instead of paying for it; usually means doing any odd jobs that the owner agrees for you to do in lieu of paying for your stay. Typically done at hostels and the White Mountain huts.

Yo-yo-ing: Term used to describe completing a thru-hike, and then turning around and completing it *again* in the other direction.

Yogi-ing: An act of "letting" food or help be offered to a thru-hiker without actually asking for it. For example, in a convenience store you are next to a person who came in with a car, and you talk loudly to your hiker friend about wishing you could get a lift back to the trail (hoping the person with the car will offer you a ride).

Zero: A day off from hiking, literally meaning zero miles hiked that day.

VIII: ACKNOWLEDGMENTS

In the end, no one finishes a thru-hike without the help or friendship of others. The same could be said with writing this book. Special thanks are in order for the following badass people.

Thanks to Jennifer Evans, editor extraordinaire. Mere words cannot describe my thanks and appreciation of you! I value your expertise, wisdom and intelligence. I look up to you, more than you know.

Thank you to these amazing women who each provided a unique perspective of hiking the Appalachian Trail: Celia, Manuela Jay, Liz Kidder, Jessica Rakestraw, Bekah Quirin, Erin Bogert, Nichole Young, Deborah Griffin, Jennifer Cenker, Jessa Victor, and Kim DeGrazia. I am lucky to have each of you as part of my book.

Thanks to Stacia Bennet for your amazing story at the end of the bonus section. Thanks to Rhesia Baron for your input in the Safety chapter. Thanks to Karen Youngs for contributing to the Fears chapter.

Thanks to my beta readers: Sara Spittle, Estee Hammer, and Lynette Hunt. All of you helped me in different ways and I'm grateful to each of you.

Thanks to Nicholas Bradley for the amazing cover of my book. You are a phenomenal artist!

And my Greg. I honestly don't know where I'd be in this life without you. You constantly push me to be the best I can be.

You listen. You understand. You are always on my side. Also, thanks for getting me off my ass in the first place and telling me to start writing down my ideas for a woman's book!

IX: ABOUT THE AUTHOR

Defying the mantra *work more, spend more,* Jen stepped off the corporate treadmill in 2013 and moved with her husband to Costa Rica. With time to pursue her passions, she learned to live simply and meaningfully. She wrote several books on Costa Rica and developed a fondness for hiking in the mountains of the Central Valley.

After four years of *pura vida* (pure life) in Costa Rica, Jen and Greg decided it was time to hit the road again and take a hike – literally – on the Appalachian Trail. Through daily vlogs on YouTube, Jen and Greg recorded their six-month, adventure of a lifetime from Springer Mountain, Georgia to Mount Katahdin, Maine.

After finishing their trek, Jen co-authored *Thru-Hiking the Appalachian Trail – 100 Tips, Tricks, Traps, and Facts* with her husband. Jen also has a successful jewelry business – including a line of hiking jewelry.

Most recently, Jen and Greg completed the Camino de Santiago, a 500-mile pilgrimage across northern Spain – check out their YouTube for recent daily vlogs – and are currently contemplating "what's next."

Jen's Arm Candy: CostaRicaChicaArmCandy.com
Facebook: Facebook.com/ChicaandSunsets
Instagram: Instagram.com/ChicaandSunsets
YouTube: YouTube.com/ChicaandSunsets
Blog: ChicaandSunscts.com
Jen's Books: Amazon.com (search under "Jen Beck Seymour")

Made in the USA
Columbia, SC
06 October 2021

46811135R00178